Every

Everyman, I
and b

Dante

Selected and edited by ANNA LAWRENCE

EVERYMAN

J. M. Dent · London

This edition first published by Everyman Paperbacks in 1998
Introduction and other critical apparatus
© J. M. Dent 1998

J. M. Dent
Orion Publishing Group
Orion House
5 Upper St Martin's Lane
London WC2H 9EA

Typeset by Deltatype Ltd, Birkenhead, Merseyside
Printed in Great Britain by
The Guernsey Press Co. Ltd, Guernsey, C. I.

British Library Cataloguing-in-Publication
Data is available upon request.

ISBN 0 460 87955 3

Contents

From *The Divine Comedy*: *Hell*   13

Early *Rime*   27

The Banquet   33

Note on the Author and Editor

DANTE was born, in May 1265, into a comfortably-off mercantile family; the business had been established by Dante's grandfather, Bellincione, and passed to Alighiero II, Bellincione's first son and Dante's father. Alighiero, whose pragmatism as a businessman earned him a dubious reputation as money-lender and usurer, married twice, first to Bella who died young, and shortly after to Lapa di Chiarissimo Cialuffi. Dante was Bella's first-born; he had a sister and two half-siblings from Alighiero's second marriage. The family was of White Guelph allegiance and could trace its roots back to Cacciaguida (see *Paradise*, canto 17) the Crusader-knight who married Aldighiera, with whom the family name originated.

Dante married Gemma Donati in 1285 and had by her three children: Pietro, Jacopo and Antonia. The marriage was an arranged one (Dante and Gemma had been betrothed since 1277), and was never terribly happy. There are rumours of another son, Giovanni, and moreover, Dante's lifelong love, figuring centrally in the *New Life* and the *Comedy*, was for Beatrice Portinari.

By 1300, Dante, now head of the family business and an established poet, is politically engaged. On 13 June he is elected as one of the six ruling Priors of Florence and is immediately involved in the banishment of both Black and White Guelphs for rioting. (Among the latter group, was his great friend and fellow poet Guido Cavalcanti, who died in exile). The political situation worsened with increased divisions between the Black Guelphs supported by the Pope, and Dante's White faction. In November 1301, while Dante was returning from a diplomatic mission to Rome, a *coup d'état* saw the Black Guelphs return to power in Florence. Members of the former ruling class were banished; Dante never returned to Florence.

He spent the remainder of his years in the precarious position of an exile, working as diplomat and mediator for a variety of patrons and producing the bulk of his literary work. In 1318 he moved from the court and protection of Cangrande della Scala at Verona to the literary court of Guido Novello da Polenta, poet and potentate of

Ravenna. Here, surrounded by his family (Antonia had taken the veil in a convent nearby and his sons were present at the court), he continued his diplomatic and literary career. In 1321 Guido sent him on a diplomatic mission to the State of Venice to dissuade the Venetians from waging war on Ravenna. On the outward journey, Dante contracted what may have been malaria and died, shortly after returning to Ravenna, on 14 September. He was buried in the church of San Francesco; Guido's plan to build a monument was thwarted by political events and repeated requests by the Florentines for return of the bones led the Franciscan monks to hide them in a boundary wall. They were found only in 1865, and transferred to the eighteenth-century monument in which they still lie.

Following research at the University of Cambridge, ANNA LAWRENCE has lectured at the Universities of Birmingham and Warwick. Now based in London, she is working on a number of research and editing projects.

Chronology of Dante's Life

Year	Life
1265	Born in Florence between 4 May and 13 June to Alighiero II and Bella
1266	Beatrice is born; she is nine or ten months younger than Dante
	26 February: Battle of Benevento with the help of Charles of Anjou, the Guelphs defeat the Imperial army
	26 March (Holy Saturday): Dante baptised as Durante
1267	Guelph rule restored in Florence
1269	Dante's grandfather, Bellincione, last mentioned as *intra vivos*
1274	May? Dante sees Beatrice for the first time
1277	9 January: contract for betrothal of Gemma Donati to Dante is drawn up
1280	Geri del Bello, a cousin of Dante's father, murdered
1281/1282	Perhaps even the beginning of 1283, Dante's father dies – of natural causes or murder? He may also have been excommunicated, for heresy or usury
1283	Sees Beatrice again
	Starts to correspond with his fellow poet, Guido Cavalcanti
1285	Dante marries Gemma Donati
1287	Beatrice marries
	Birth of Dante's first child: Pietro; followed by Jacopo and Antonia
1289	11 June: Dante fights at the battle of Campaldino at which Ghibelline forces are defeated
	Folco di Ricovero Portinari, Beatrice's father, dies 31 December
1290	Beatrice dies 8 or 9 June
1292–1293	Possible date for composition of *New Life*

1294   Abdication of Pope Celestine V; Boniface VIII elected

1296   July: the poet Forese Donati dies (See *Purgatory*, canto 26)

        Dante is actively engaged in Florentine political affairs

1300   Year of Jubilee proclaimed by Boniface VIII

        13 June: Dante elected as one of six Priors in Florence – the highest office of the Florentine State. Period of office lasts from 15 June – 15 August

        23 June: the Priors punish rioting between Black and White Guelphs by banishment of members of both factions; Dante's friend and fellow poet Guido Cavalcanti is amongst them

        August: Cavalcanti dies of malaria in exile in Sarzana

1301   19 June: Dante speaks out against sending 100 knights to help the Pope fight Margherita Aldobrandeschi (See notes to *Purgatory*, canto 5)

        White Guelphs are defeated; 1st November Charles of Valois enters Florence; 7th November black Guelph junta takes power; Dante, returning from a spell as Florentine ambassador to Rome, hears of accusations of corruption levelled against him

1302   27 January: the new administration condemns, *in absentia*, former Florentine leaders to permanent exclusion from public office, a fine of 5,000 Florins and banishment for two years on false charges of fraud and corruption. The accused refuse to pay or present themselves before the authorities

        10 March: a second edict sentences Dante and 14 co-accused to be burned alive if ever they venture into Florentine territory again

        Autumn: stays with the Lord of Forlì

1303   Earliest possible date for initiation of *De Vulgari Eloquentia*. First stay in Verona perhaps until March 1304 (See notes to *Paradise*, canto 17)

        Boniface VIII dies; Benedict XI elected in his stead

1304   7 July: Pope Benedict XI dies

        20 July: defeat of the alliance of exiled

        Florentines at Val di Mugnone; Petrarch born the same day

1304–1307	Probable date for composition of the prose part of *The Banquet*; Dante may be staying in Treviso over this period
1305	5 June: Clement V elected Pope. Dante may have met Giotto and seen the Scrovegni Chapel during this year, or in 1304
1306	6 October: Dante on his way to Castelnuovo as peacemaker working for the Malaspina family
1307	Possibly in the Casentino, and then, perhaps, in Lucca until beginning of 1309
	Dante may start composition of *Comedy*
1309–1310	Possibly in Paris
1311–1312	Dante may have completed the *Purgatory*
1312	Dante might be beginning *The Monarchy* – a manifesto of political philosophy, written in Latin. Other evidence suggests, however, this may have been composed as late as 1318
1313	Birth of Boccaccio
	24 August: Henry VII dies at Buonconvento
1314	Dante stays for six years with Cangrande della Scala at Verona
	Probable date of publication of first part of *Comedy*: *Hell*
	20 April: Pope Clement V dies: interregnum until 1316
1315	May: the Florentine authorities grant amnesty to the exiles – Dante refuses the terms which demand part-payment of the fine and acknowledgement of guilt. The whole family is subsequently condemned to death, their property confiscated and destroyed
	Autumn: probable date of publication of second part of *Comedy*: *Purgatory*
1316	Probably engaged in composition of third part of *Comedy*: *Paradise*
	John XXII elected Pope
1318	Moves to Ravenna

1320   20 January: on the way back from Mantua delivers
        lecture – *Quaestio de acqua et terra* – a treatise on
        natural science – in Church at Verona
        Correspondence with Giovanni del Virgilio

1321   Diplomatic mission to Venice to dissuade the
        Venetians from waging war on Ravenna in
        retaliation for the predations of the Ravennese ships
        upon the Venetian fleet; contracts malaria(?) on
        outward journey
        14 September: Dante dies at Ravenna

Introduction

Dante Alighieri is one of those authors whose work is inseparable from the historical context in which he lived, but for whom historical detail is far from providing an answer to his complexities or anything other than partial elucidation of the more perplexing moments of his *oeuvre*. In fact, our knowledge of him is full of gaps; nothing is left to us written in his own hand, the last part of his great narrative poem, the *Comedy*, was nearly lost, his movements when in exile are far from clear (he may even have visited Oxford), and some of the works attributed to him are of dubious authorship. Moreover, the modern non-specialist reader is unlikely to associate his name with anything other than the first part of the *Comedy*, the *Inferno*, or *Hell*, which has earned him the nickname 'the great hater' – an epithet which could scarcely be more mistaken in its intended criticism. For the author of *Hell* is the author also of the *Purgatory* and *Paradise*, the great envisionings, humane and full of hope, of the other two realms of the afterlife.

But this is to leap forwards to the latter half of Dante's life and literary output. For despite the horrendous images he offers us in Hell, or the apparently rarefied theology of Heaven, Dante first makes his name as a love poet. He is born, however, into a mercantile family, to a business established by his grandfather Bellincione and cultivated by his father Alighiero II. When, on the death of his father between 1281 and 1283, Dante as first born becomes head of both family and business, it also becomes apparent that Bellincione's business links with the Florentine nobility had benefited his grandson by providing him with a more expensive, more upper-class education, with well-connected contacts and with a taste for fine living, but not with much interest in or instinct for commercial dealings. In fact, Dante's skills are to be in other more literary, political and diplomatic fields and his half-brother, Francesco, eventually takes over the business. But Bellincione had imparted to Dante his own Guelph allegiances. The division between Guelph and Ghibelline, the former supporting the secular power of the papacy and the latter advocating the rule of the emperor and the restriction of the Pope to spiritual affairs, was crucial to Italian politics and Dante's own history. By 1295, Dante entered Florentine politics on the Guelph side – the very year that the Guelphs were fatally to split into two factions, the aggressively pro-papal Blacks and the more moderate Whites with whom Dante sided. It was from this point on that Bellincione's ability to establish connections was to come to the fore in his grandson's life as, involved now in politics, Dante met and worked with the foremost personalities of the time, people like Nino Visconti, Charles Martel, Corso Donati, the Donateschi clan, the Cavalcantis, Henry VII, Boniface VIII.

The public and the political grew out of the personal, family history. This duality is reflected throughout Dante's work, and it is focused in Dante's relation with the Cavalcanti family. Originating in France or Germany, the Cavalcantis were among the founders of Florentine Guelphism and, before the Alighieri counted for anything, were central to the city's history. Events and allegiances of the personal and political variety begin to collide with the potency of fissile material by the summer of 1300 when, as Prior, Dante was involved in exiling Black and White Guelphs for rioting. Among the latter group was the major cultural figure, leading poet and Dante's closest friend, Guido Cavalcanti. Guido died in exile and was not to see Dante's own fall from power just over a year later in an exile and death sentence, confirmed in 1315, and extended to the whole of his immediate family.

The years before this calamity had however, through the friendship, rivalry and correspondence with Guido Cavalcanti and with other poets, seen Dante establish himself as a foremost love poet. He wrote as one of the *stilnovisti* (the poets of the new style), a group of Tuscan and Emilian authors who most fully discussed the ambiguities of love: its capacity to strike – even destructively – at the lover's inmost being, its tendency to possess and obsess, its unrequitedness. The stilnovist aesthetic was evident stylistically, in clarity of expression, grace and musicality; and in substance, in a philosophy of love not about possession, but about a progress towards self-transcendence, where love engenders an openness to the other and through them, to goodness and to the highest form of human being.

Stilnovismo was itself a refinement of the courtly love tradition that developed quite suddenly in eleventh-century France. Here, in Languedoc, love was modelled on the feudal court and, in the brutality of feudal society, the beloved was the sole source of manners and gentleness, the feudal Lord's Lady. And the lover was her servant, always obedient to her requests, silent at her rebukes, unquestioning at her inevitable rejection. But this of course meant that love was inevitably adulterous and unrealisable – and this, admitted or denied, was the central problem around which all love poetry revolved. It was no different for Dante who, established as a poet already from 1283, produced his first unified work before he was thirty. This was the *New Life*, a little book drawn together from some of his early poems newly surrounded by a prose framework fitting them together in a narrative and literary-critical order. It tells the story of Dante's love for Beatrice whom he first sees when they are both nine – and nine is a Trinity of Trinities, a miraculous number. Of Beatrice we know very little except that she was probably Beatrice Portinari, she died in 1290, she was never even betrothed to Dante and in fact married two years after he did.

Closely involved in the contradictions of his tradition, Dante's unrivalled capacity to turn a personal problem inside out, to bring the private difficulty to public relevance, becomes evident in the development of his early poems and in the compilation of the *New Life*. Rather than ignoring or accepting the ethical dilemma, he overturns outworn literary conventions and comes to see love as the principle of intellectual and ethical being. The *New Life* is not just self-explanation, but explanation of the greater question of the human experience of love; and though open-ended in its conclusion, it establishes a quite new idea, that through love, guided by reason, Man can reach his highest happiness. Dante's preoccupation with love as central question drives his invention of the sweet new style, the praise style, even the bitter style or *stile aspro*. It is love which leads to the moral and spiritual regeneration of the lover, and the questions raised by love impart to Dante's poetry the dialectical energy that characterises many of his exchanges with other poets.

It is in the tradition of courtly love that Dante da Maiano writes an exchange of epistolary sonnets with Dante Alighieri. *Wisdom and courtesy, genius and art* (page 27) is the final poem in that series and is written in reply to da Maiano's *Amor mi fa sì fedelmente amare*. Dante da Maiano's poem goes something like this:

> So faithfully Love makes me love
> And so closely holds in his desire,

> That I could not an hour retire
> My heart from thinking on true love.
> [....]
> I fully know and truly now
> That versus Love prevails nor force nor art
> Nor plan nor spell that man can find,
> But mercy and long suffering and how
> To serve the Lady well; this is the lover's part.
> See now, wise friend, if I have to truth my pen inclined.

Alighieri's answer was not as approving as da Maiano might have hoped. Where the latter is confined to the old tropes of courtly love, in which the unrequited lover remains passive and where dogged persistence and service are all, Alighieri combines intellect and ethics to come to a new understanding of love: it is undeniably part of human experience and love poetry is its constructive expression.

> Wisdom and courtesy, genius and art,
> Beauty and wealth, and true nobility,
> [. . .]
> Virtues and graces are that everywhere
> By their sweet power of pleasing conquer Love.
> [. . .]
> Hence if thou wish, my friend, to make avail
> Thy virtues, whether native or acquired,
> Employ them loyally in pleasing Love;
> Never oppose his gracious ministry,
> Assured that nothing can defend the man
> Who wages battle wilfully with him.

Wisdom and courtesy . . . is one of the early *Rime* (poems), one that was not selected as part of the *New Life*. The sonnet reveals a practical response to love that remains central throughout Dante's *œuvre*. Even by the time he writes the *Comedy*, those in Hell lose *the good of intellect* because they have no understanding of love; but to gaze at God face to face as the protagonist does at the end of *Paradise*, is to understand *the Love which moves the sun and the other stars*. And at the beginning of his literary career, the private and confessional *New Life* also aims at establishing a more public intellectual and stylistic coherence: an order, not just of development, but a system in which understanding can flourish. Its title is therefore deliberate in its Pauline echo: true understanding of love constitutes a 'newness of life', the first glimpses of what a human being can be, of genuinely human becoming.

The praise style, of which the poem *My lady looks so gentle and so pure* is perhaps the finest single example, is a further stage in this process. Here, the characteristic of the *New Life* poems as linguistic and spiritual meditations, is most obvious. Beatrice, who is also, etymologically, the one who gives blessing, becomes an epiphany: a revealer of other possibilities and of realities beyond the self. The poem, with its sister sonnet *For certain he hath seen all perfectness*, develops the stilnovist notion of the Lady as ennobling force, even as Maker. Through etymological links, her salutation gains the power to confer salvation and 'through her, [hers] are raised above'. Dante is refining a philosophy of love in which love rises beyond its necessarily adulterous origins in the courtly tradition, and circumvents the problematic surrounding sexual desire. The vigorous intellectual and spiritual meditation that is the *New Life*, renews the language of love poetry and provides a fresh understanding of what it is to be human. And the culmination of the book in the sonnet *Beyond the sphere which spreads to widest space*, marks an ascent of mind out of whose 'new perception' is to come, says Dante, *quello che mai non fu detto d'alcuna:* 'what hath not before been written of any woman'.

It may be that this is already a foreshadowing of the *Comedy* which Dante began to compose in exile after his lyric poetry had been written and some of it selected for the *New Life* and *The Banquet*. But after the Black Guelph *coup* and his banishment on fabricated charges, until his death in 1321, Dante supported himself and his family by using his political and diplomatic skills in the service of a variety of patrons. Already a well-known poet, his presence in the courts of his patrons had an additional cachet, but there is evidence that Francesco had to intervene on a number of occasions to support his half-brother financially. Throughout his exile, Dante characteristically turns questions and calamities that troubled him personally into works of general relevance. And this is so at every point of Dante's vastly diverse output: a spirit of enormous generosity turns outwards from private experience towards the public good. The Latin treatise on Italian vernacular, *De vulgari eloquentia*, is written 'to aid the language of the common people' and thereby identify an 'illustrious vernacular' which might also transcend the political divisions of the time. The Latin

Monarchy, a political work evidencing Dante's move towards Ghibellinism in its argument for a Universal Ruler, starts by enunciating the principle that all men who love the truth must work for future generations and contribute to the common good. *The Banquet* meanwhile, is written for those who are too busy to study for themselves: this encyclopaedic work is dedicated to others because 'all Men naturally desire to know'.

The Banquet was never finished, and Dante only uses three of possibly fifteen intended poems, placing prose commentaries once again around verse. The commentary for the second poem *Love, who discourses to me in my mind*, was written perhaps ten years after the verse original. It explains the canzone as the praise of Philosophy, allegorised as a lady who takes pride of place in Dante's affections after the death of Beatrice. But this Philosophy, defined elsewhere as 'the loving use of wisdom', has a countenance that shows *the ineffable delights of Paradise*; her eyes, according to the commentary, are the 'eyes of wisdom' which 'are her demonstrations, [. . .] and her smile is her persuasions'. And it is of secondary importance that this canzone is one of Dante's great allegorical poems, for from a love of philosophy which engenders *The Banquet* and which the book is concerned to share, there develops also, inseparably, a philosophy of love. As Dante says, 'love is the necessary condition for doing philosophy'.

> And so I say: 'On her all heaven's intelligences gaze', and I say 'heaven's intelligences' relating them to God, whom I have mentioned before; but I am excluding the intelligences which have been exiled from on high, who cannot philosophise, since in them all love is spent – and being able to *love is the necessary condition for doing philosophy*. So, you see, the infernal intelligences cannot gaze on this beautiful lady: and since she is the very blessing of the intellect, their privation of her is full of bitterness and of every kind of sadness. [. . .] And I have said before, if you remember, that *love is the form of philosophy*, so here love is called her soul: and this love is manifested in the use of wisdom which leads to wonderful things such as contentment in every condition of life, and scorn for the idols others set up as their gods.

This conviction that a practical understanding of love results in the performative *doing* of philosophy, runs through everything that Dante wrote. Even the *Comedy* was not created fully formed, *ex nihilo*. Dante's philosophy of love contributes centrally to this too. The commentary to the third canzone of *The Banquet* illuminates one of the episodes in *Hell* which is also part of our selection. The canzone is a doctrinal poem concerned with the definition of nobility. Dante sets this civic virtue in a moral context: nobility, he says, is not derived from inherited wealth and lineage, but from our choices and our actions, and this capacity for self-determination on a moral plane, is essential to our humanity. To fail to use it is fatal to our reason, and without reason what remains 'is no longer a man'; 'such vile people', Dante sustains, 'are dead even though they seem to be alive'. The undead of *Hell* 33, Branca d'Oria and Frate Alberigo, are examples of the deadening effect of sin, or, more comprehensibly, that what we do effects how we exist. According to Dante 'the use of reason is essential to human life, [. . .] to stray from that use is to abandon being and so to become dead'. The choices that Alberigo and Branca d'Oria make are so morally unreasonable that their evil is irreparable: they have clearly abandoned the defining human capacity for moral choice and they become undead.

The *Comedy* is not, therefore, about the afterlife as such, but about dispositions and activity in *this* life – even if seen via the next. It is the culmination of Dante's philosophy of love, and reveals ways in which human beings may live well, or badly; it is centrally concerned, therefore, with the business of being human, with human *being* in the most performative sense. Brunetto, Branca d'Oria, Ugolino, as opposed to the more authentically human Buonconte or Guinizelli or Adam, are people who have chosen not to make, but unmake themselves. There is no sense, as there is for instance in one of the later poems, *Three ladies have retreated to my heart*, that personal tragedy may be opened outwards, turned to the public good. None of these individuals could 'banishment an honour deem', nor sing, in the language of a love poem, of Justice and Law. Buonconte falls in battle with the name of a Lady – the Virgin Mary – on his lips, but for no soul in Hell was self-transcendence or openness to the other ever actualised. For their separate reasons, each has chosen not to see the good beyond themselves, not to be led, as Dante is by Beatrice and as the souls of Purgatory and Paradise are, to that *Love which moves the sun and the other stars*.

ANNA LAWRENCE

Note on the Text

The poems selected for this anthology are drawn from the whole of Dante's lyric poetry and include cantos from each of the three parts of the *Comedy*. The translations of poems from the *New Life* are by Dante Gabriel Rossetti, as is one of Dante's early poems, 'Upon a day, came Sorrow in to me' (p. 33). Other translations of lyric poetry are by Charles Lyell, with two poems, 'By reason of a garland fair' (p. 30) and 'Ye words of mine, whose voice the world doth fill' (p. 58), by E H Plumptre. The selections from *Hell* are in the new translation by Robert Pinsky, and those of the *Purgatory* and *Paradise* from the classic translations of H F Carey and Longfellow respectively. It should be added that passages such as Byron's translation in *Don Juan* (III. cviii) of the first eight lines of *Purgatory* 8, Shelley's recreation in *The Triumph of Life* (line 176ff) of *Hell* 32: 85–102, or Eliot's version of *Hell* 15 from *Little Gidding*, are not included here – being for a very different volume than the present one.

Dante Alighieri

From *The New Life*

A ciascun' alma presa e gentil core

To every heart which the sweet pain doth move,
    And unto which these words may now be brought
    For true interpretation and kind thought,
Be greeting in our Lord's name, which is Love.
Of those long hours wherein the stars, above,
    Wake and keep watch, the third was almost nought,
    When Love was shown me with such terrors fraught
As may not carelessly be spoken of.
He seemed like one who is full of joy, and had
    My heart within his hand, and on his arm   10
My lady, with a mantle round her, slept;
Whom (having wakened her) anon he made
    To eat that heart; she ate, as fearing harm.
    Then he went out; and as he went, he wept.

Ballata, i' voi che tu ritrovi Amore

Song, 'tis my will that thou do seek out Love,
    And go with him where my dear lady is;
    That so my cause, the which thy harmonies
Do plead, his better speech may clearly prove.

Thou goest, my Song, in such a courteous kind,
    That even companionless
        Thou mayst rely on thyself anywhere.
And yet, an thou wouldst get thee a safe mind,
    First unto Love address
        Thy steps; whose aid, mayhap, 'twere ill to spare,   10

Seeing that she to whom thou mak'st thy prayer
Is, as I think, ill-minded unto me,
And that if Love do not companion thee,
    Thou'lt have perchance small cheer to tell me of.

With a sweet accent, when thou com'st to her,
    Begin thou in these words,
        First having craved a gracious audience:
'He who hath sent me as his messenger,
Lady, thus much records,
    An thou but suffer him, in his defence.   20
    Love, who comes with me, by thine influence
Can make this man do as it liketh him:
Wherefore, if this fault *is* or doth but *seem*
    Do thou conceive: for his heart cannot move.'

Say to her also: 'Lady, his poor heart
    Is so confirmed in faith
        That all its thoughts are but of serving thee
'Twas early thine, and could not swerve apart.'
    Then, if she wavereth,
        Bid her ask Love, who knows if these things be.   30
        And in the end, beg of her modestly
To pardon so much boldness: saying too:—
'If thou declare his death to be thy due,
    The thing shall come to pass, as doth behove.'

Then pray thou of the Master of all ruth,
    Before thou leave her there,
        That he befriend my cause and plead it well.
'In guerdon of my sweet rhymes and my truth'
    (Entreat him) 'stay with her;
        Let not the hope of thy poor servant fail;   40
        And if with her thy pleading should prevail,
Let her look on him and give peace to him.'
Gentle my Song, if good to thee it seem,
    Do this: so worship shall be thine and love.

Con l'altre donne mia vista gabbate

Even as the others mock, thou mockest me;
   Not dreaming, noble lady, whence it is
   That I am taken with strange semblances,
Seeing thy face which is so fair to see:
For else, compassion would not suffer thee
   To grieve my heart with such harsh scoffs as these.
   Lo! Love, when thou art present, sits at ease,
And bears his mastership so mightily
That all my troubled senses he thrusts out,
   Sorely tormenting some, and slaying some,   10
     Till none but he is left and has free range
     To gaze on thee. This makes my face to change
   Into another's; while I stand all dumb,
And hear my senses clamour in the their rout.

Donne ch'avete intelletto d'amore

Ladies that have intelligence in love,
   Of mine own lady I would speak with you;
   Not that I hope to count her praises through,
     But telling what I may, to ease my mind.
And I declare that when I speak thereof,
Love sheds such perfect sweetness over me
That if my courage failed not, certainly
     To him my listeners must be all resign'd.
     Wherefore I will not speak in such large kind
That mine own speech should foil me, which were
     base;   10
But only will discourse of her high grace
     In these poor words, the best that I can find,
With you alone, dear dames and damozels:
'Twere ill to speak thereof with any else.

An Angel, of his blessed knowledge, saith
  To God: 'Lord, in the world that Thou hast made,
  A miracle in action is display'd,
    By reason of a soul whose splendours fare
Even hither: and since Heaven requireth
  Nought saving her, for her it prayeth Thee,   20
  Thy Saints crying aloud continually.'
    Yet Pity still defends our earthly share
    In that sweet soul; God answering thus the prayer.
'My well-belovèd, suffer that in peace
Your hope remain, while so My pleasure is,
  There where one dwells who dreads the loss of her:
And who in Hell unto the doomed shall say,
"I have looked on that for which God's chosen pray." '

My lady is desired in the high Heaven:
  Wherefore, it now behoveth me to tell,   30
  Saying: Let any maid that would be well
    Esteemed keep with her: for as she goes by,
Into foul hearts a deathly chill is driven
By Love, that makes ill thought to perish there:
While any who endures to gaze on her
    Must either be ennobled, or else die.
    When one deserving to be raised so high
Is found, 'tis then her power attains its proof,
Making his heart strong for his soul's behoof
    With the full strength of meek humility.   40
    Also this virtue owns she, by God's will:
Who speaks with her can never come to ill.

Love saith concerning her: 'How chanceth it
  That flesh, which is of dust, should be thus pure?'
  Then, gazing always, he makes oath: 'Forsure,
    This is a creature of God till now unknown.'
She hath that paleness of the pearl that's fit
In a fair woman, so much and not more;
She is as high as Nature's skill can soar;
    Beauty is tried by her comparison.   50
    Whatever her sweet eyes are turned upon,
Spirits of love do issue thence in flame,

Which through their eyes who then may look on them
   Pierce to the heart's deep chamber every one.
And in her smile Love's image you may see;
Whence none can gaze upon her steadfastly.

Dear Song, I know thou wilt hold gentle speech
   With many ladies, when I send thee forth:
   Wherefore (being mindful that thou hadst thy birth
      From Love, and art a modest, simple child,)   60
Whomso thou meetest, say thou this to each:
'Give me good speed! To her I wend along
In whose much strength my weakness is made strong.'
      And if i' the end, thou wouldst not be beguiled
      Of all thy labour, seek not the defiled
And common sort; but rather choose to be
Where man and woman dwell in courtesy.
      So to the road thou shalt be reconciled,
And find the lady, and with the lady, Love.
Commend thou me to each, as doth behove.   70

Amore e 'l cor gentil sono una cosa

Love and the gentle heart are one same thing,
   Even as the wise man in his ditty saith:
   Each, of itself, would be such life in death
As rational soul bereft of reasoning.
'Tis Nature makes them when she loves: a king
   Love is, whose palace where he sojourneth
   Is called the Heart; there draws he quiet breath
At first, with brief or longer slumbering.
Then beauty seen in virtuous womankind
   Will make the eyes desire, and through the heart   10
      Send the desiring of the eyes again;
Where often it abides so long enshrin'd
   That Love at length out of his sleep will start.
     And women feel the same for worthy men.

Ne li occhi porta la mia donna Amore

My lady carries love within her eyes;
   All that she looks on is made pleasanter;
   Upon her path men turn to gaze at her;
He whom she greeteth feels his heart to rise,
And droops his troubled visage, full of sighs,
   And of his evil heart is then aware:
   Hate loves, and pride becomes a worshipper.
O women, help to praise her in somewise.
Humbleness, and the hope that hopeth well,
   By speech of hers into the mind are brought,   10
     And who beholds is blessèd oftenwhiles.
     The look she hath when she a little smiles
Cannot be said, nor holden in the thought;
'Tis such a new and gracious miracle.

Donna pietosa e di novella etate

A very pitiful Lady, very young,
   Exceeding rich in human sympathies,
     Stood by, what time I clamour'd upon Death;
And at the wild words wandering on my tongue
   And at the piteous look within mine eyes
     She was affrighted, that sobs choked her breath.
     So by her weeping where I lay beneath,
Some other gentle ladies came to know
My state, and made her go:
Afterward, bending themselves over me,   10
One said, 'Awaken thee!'
     And one, 'What thing thy sleep disquieteth?'
With that, my soul woke up from its eclipse,
The while my lady's name rose to my lips:

But utter'd in a voice so sob-broken,
   So feeble with the agony of tears,

That I alone might hear it in my heart;
And though that look was on my visage then
  Which he who is ashamed so plainly wears,
    Love made that I through shame held not apart,   20
    But gazed upon them. And my hue was such
That they look'd at each other and thought of death;
Saying under their breath
Most tenderly, 'O let us comfort him:'
Then unto me: 'What dream
  Was thine, that it hath shaken thee so much?'
And when I was a little comforted,
'This, ladies, was the dream I dreamt,' I said.

'I was a-thinking how life fails with us
  Suddenly after such a little while;   30
    When Love sobb'd in my heart, which is his home.
Whereby my spirit wax'd so dolorous
  That in myself I said, with sick recoil:
    "Yea, to my lady too this Death must come."
    And therewithal such a bewilderment
Possess'd me, that I shut mine eyes for peace;
And in my brain did cease
Order of thought, and every healthful thing.
Afterwards, wandering
  Amid a swarm of doubts that came and went,   40
Some certain women's faces hurried by,
And shriek'd to me, "Thou too shalt die, shalt die!"

'Then saw I many broken hinted sights
  In the uncertain state I stepp'd into.
    Meseem'd to be I know not in what place,
Where ladies through the street, like mournful lights,
  Ran with loose hair, and eyes that frighten'd you
    By their own terror, and a pale amaze:
    The while, little by little, as I thought,
The sun ceased, and the stars began to gather,   50
And each wept at the other;
And birds dropp'd in mid-flight out of the sky;
And earth shook suddenly;
    And I was 'ware of one, hoarse and tired out,

Who ask'd of me: "Hast thou not heard it said? . .
Thy lady, she that was so fair, is dead."

'Then lifting up mine eyes, as the tears came,
 I saw the Angels, like a rain of manna,
  In a long flight flying back Heavenward;
Having a little cloud in front of them,   60
 After the which they went and said, "Hosanna";
  And if they had said more, you should have heard.
  Then Love said, "Now shall all things be made
   clear:
Come and behold our lady where she lies."
These 'wildering phantasies
Then carried me to see my lady dead.
Even as I there was led,
 Her ladies with a veil were covering her;
And with her was such very humbleness
That she appeared to say, "I am at peace."   70

'And I became so humble in my grief,
 Seeing in her such deep humility,
  That I said: "Death, I hold thee passing good
Henceforth, and a most gentle sweet relief,
 Since my dear love has chosen to dwell with thee:
  Pity, not hate, is thine, well understood.
  Lo! I do so desire to see thy face
That I am like as one who nears the tomb;
My soul entreats thee, Come."
Then I departed, having made my moan;   80
And when I was alone
 I said, and cast my eyes to the High Place:
"Blessed is he, fair soul, who meets thy glance!"
. . . Just then you woke me, of your complaisaùnce.'

Tanto gentile e tanto onesta pare

My lady looks so gentle and so pure
　　When yielding salutation by the way,
　　That the tongue trembles and has nought to say,
And the eyes, which fain would see, may not endure.
And still, amid the praise she hears secure,
　　She walks with humbleness for her array;
　　Seeming a creature sent from Heaven to stay
On earth, and show a miracle made sure.
She is so pleasant in the eyes of men
That through the sight the inmost heart doth gain　　　　　10
　　A sweetness which needs proof to know it by:
And from between her lips there seems to move
A soothing essence that is full of love,
　　Saying for ever to the spirit, 'Sigh!'

Vede perfettamente onne salute

For certain he hath seen all perfectness
　　Who among other ladies hath seen mine:
　　They that go with her humbly should combine
To thank their God for such peculiar grace.
So perfect is the beauty of her face
　　That it begets in no wise any sign
　　Of envy, but draws round her a clear line
Of love, and blessed faith, and gentleness.
Merely the sight of her makes all things bow:
　　Not she herself alone is holier　　　　　　　　　10
　　　　Than all; but hers, through her, are raised above.
From all her acts such lovely graces flow
　　That truly one may never think of her
　　　　Without a passion of exceeding love.

Oltre la spera che più larga gira

Beyond the sphere which spreads to widest space
   Now soars the sigh that my heart sends above;
   A new perception born of grieving Love
Guideth it upward the untrodden ways.
When it hath reached unto the end, and stays,
   It sees a lady round whom splendours move
   In homage; till, by the great light thereof
Abashed, the pilgrim spirit stands at gaze.
It sees her such, that when it tells me this
   Which it hath seen, I understand it not,   10
     It hath a speech so subtile and so fine.
  And yet I know its voice within my thought
Often remembereth me of Beatrice:
     So that I understand it, ladies mine.

From *The Divine Comedy*:

Hell

CANTO 3

THROUGH ME YOU ENTER INTO THE CITY OF WOES,
  THROUGH ME YOU ENTER INTO ETERNAL PAIN,
  THROUGH ME YOU ENTER THE POPULATION OF LOSS.

JUSTICE MOVED MY HIGH MAKER, IN POWER DIVINE,
  WISDOM SUPREME, LOVE PRIMAL. NO THINGS WERE
  BEFORE ME NOT ETERNAL; ETERNAL I REMAIN.

ABANDON ALL HOPE, YOU WHO ENTER HERE.
  These words I saw inscribed in some dark colour
  Over a portal. 'Master,' I said, 'make clear

Their meaning, which I find too hard to gather.'   10
  Then he, as one who understands: 'All fear
  Must be left here, and cowardice die. Together,

We have arrived where I have told you: here
  You will behold the wretched souls who've lost
  The good of intellect.' Then, with good cheer

In his expression to encourage me, he placed
  His hand on mine: so, trusting to my guide,
  I followed him among things undisclosed.

The sighs, groans and laments at first were so loud,
  Resounding through starless air, I began to weep: 20
  Strange languages, horrible screams, words imbued

With rage or despair, cries as of troubled sleep
  Or of a tortured shrillness—they rose in a coil
  Of tumult, along with noises like the slap

Of beating hands, all fused in a ceaseless flail
   That churns and frenzies that dark and timeless air
   Like sand in a whirlwind. And I, my head in a swirl

Of error, cried: 'Master, what is this I hear?
   What people are these, whom pain has overcome?'
   He: 'This is the sorrowful state of souls unsure,   30

Whose lives earned neither honour nor bad fame.
   And they are mingled with angels of that base sort
   Who, neither rebellious to God nor faithful to Him,

Chose neither side, but kept themselves apart—
   Now Heaven expels them, not to mar its splendour,
   And Hell rejects them, lest the wicked of heart

Take glory over them.' And then I: 'Master,
   What agony is it, that makes them keen their grief
   With so much force?' He: 'I will make brief answer:

They have no hope of death, but a blind life   40
   So abject, they envy any other fate.
   To all memory of them, the world is deaf.

Mercy and justice disdain them. Let us not
   Speak of them: look and pass on.' I looked again:
   A whirling banner sped at such a rate

It seemed it might never stop; behind it a train
   Of souls, so long that I would not have thought
   Death had undone so many. When more than one

I recognised had passed, I beheld the shade
   Of him who made the Great Refusal, impelled   50
   By cowardice: so at once I understood

Beyond all doubt that this was the dreary guild
   Repellent both to God and His enemies—
   Hapless ones never alive, their bare skin galled

By wasps and flies, blood trickling down the face,
　　Mingling with tears for harvest underfoot
　　By writhing maggots. Then, when I turned my eyes

Farther along our course, I could make out
　　People upon the shore of some great river.
　　'Master,' I said, 'it seems by this dim light   60

That all of these are eager to cross over—
　　Can you tell me by what law, and who they are?'
　　He answered, 'Those are things you will discover

When we have paused at Acheron's dismal shore.'
　　I walked on with my head down after that,
　　Fearful I had displeased him, and spoke no more.

Then, at the river—an old man in a boat:
　　White-haired, as he drew closer shouting at us,
　　'Woe to you, wicked souls! Give up the thought

Of Heaven! I come to ferry you across   70
　　Into eternal dark on the opposite side,
　　Into fire and ice! And you there—leave this place,

You living soul, stand clear of these who are dead!'
　　And then, when he saw that I did not obey:
　　'By other ports, in a lighter boat,' he said,

'You will be brought to shore by another way.'
　　My master spoke then, 'Charon, do not rage:
　　Thus it is willed where everything may be

Simply if it is willed. Therefore, oblige,
　　And ask no more.' That silenced the grizzled jaws   80
　　Of the gray ferryman of the livid marsh,

Who had red wheels of flame about his eyes.
　　But at his words the forlorn and naked souls
　　Were changing colour, cursing the human race,

God and their parents. Teeth chattering in their skulls,
  They called curses on the seed, the place, the hour
  Of their own begetting and their birth. With wails

And tears they gathered on the evil shore
  That waits for all who don't fear God. There demon
  Charon beckons them, with his eyes of fire;   90

Crowded in a herd, they obey if he should summon,
  And he strikes at any laggards with his oar.
  As leaves in quick succession sail down in autumn

Until the bough beholds its entire store
  Fallen to the earth, so Adam's evil seed
  Swoop from the bank when each is called, as sure

As a trained falcon, to cross to the other side
  Of the dark water; and before one throng can land
  On the far shore, on this side new souls crowd.

'My son,' said the gentle master, 'here are joined   100
  The souls of all who die in the wrath of God,
  From every country, all of them eager to find

Their way across the water—for the goad
  Of Divine Justice spurs them so, their fear
  Is transmuted to desire. Souls who are good

Never pass this way; therefore, if you hear
  Charon complaining at your presence, consider
  What that means.' Then, the earth of that grim shore

Began to shake: so violently, I shudder
  And sweat recalling it now. And wind burst up   110
  From the tear-soaked ground to erupt red light and batter

My senses—and so I fell, as though seized by sleep.

CANTO 15

Now the firm margin bears us, under the vapour
   Rising from the stream to form a shade and fend
   The fire off, sheltering both banks and water.

As Flemings between Wissant and Bruges, to defend
   Against the tide that rushes in on them,
   Construct a bulwark to drive the sea from land;

And Paduans on the Brenta do, to stem
   The water and protect their castle and town
   Before Carentana feels the heat—in the same

Manner those banks were made, except the one   10
   Who built them did not make them as high or thick,
   Whoever he was. And I could not have seen

The wood that lay behind us, had I looked back,
   When we encountered another troop of souls
   Who looked at us the way that men will look

At one another at dusk, when daylight fails
   Under a new moon: knitting their brows at us
   The way old tailors do when threading needles.

While I was being examined by them thus,
   One recognised me, and took me by the hem,   20
   Crying, 'Why what a marvel!' I fixed my eyes

On his scorched face as he reached out his arm,
   And the baked features I saw did not forestall
   My knowing him—I reached back down to him,

My hand toward his face, and answered his call:
   'Are you here, Ser Brunetto?' He replied,
   'My son, may it not displease you, if awhile

Brunetto Latini turns back to walk instead
   With you a little, and lets the train go on.'
   'I beg it of you with all my heart,' I said—   30

'And should you prefer that you and I sit down,
   If it pleases him with whom I go, I will.'
   He said, 'If any of this flock, O son,

Stops even for an instant, he must lie still
   A hundred years, not brushing off the fire
   That strikes him. Go, then: I'll follow at your heel,

And then rejoin my band who walk in a choir
   Lamenting their eternal woes.' Afraid
   To step down to his level from where we were,

I bent my head, as in reverence. He said,   40
   'What destiny or fortune makes you come
   Before your final day; and who is this guide?'

'In the bright life above,' I answered him,
   'I came into a valley and lost my way,
   Before my age had reached its ripening time—

I turned my back on the place but yesterday.
   He appeared to me at dawn, when I had turned
   To go back down, and this path is the way

By which he leads me home.' Then he returned:
   'If you keep navigating by your star   50
   You'll find a glorious port, if I discerned

Well in the fair life. Had my years been more,
   So I could witness how heaven has been kind
   To you, I would have wished your work good cheer.

But that ungrateful, malignant folk who descend
   From those brought down from Fiesole long ago,
   And who still smack of mountains and rocky ground,

Will make themselves, for good things that you do,
   Your enemies—and there is reason in that:
   Among the bitter sorb-trees, it seems undue   60

When the sweet fig in season comes to fruit.
   The world's old saying is that they are blind:
   A people greedy, envious, proud—see fit

To cleanse their habits from yourself. You'll find
   Your fortune holds such honour as will induce
   One party and the other to contend

In hunger to consume you—then the grass
   Will be well kept at a distance from the goat.
   Let the Fiesolan beasts go find their mess

By feeding on themselves, and spare the shoot   70
   (If any still should grow on their heap of dung)
   In which the sacred seed is living yet

Of Romans who remained when Florence went wrong,
   Becoming a nest for the malevolent.'
   'Could I have everything for which I long,

You would not still endure this banishment
   Away from human nature,' I replied.
   'Your image—dear, fatherly, benevolent—

Being fixed inside my memory, has imbued
   My heart: when in the fair world, hour by hour   80
   You taught me, patiently, it was you who showed

The way man makes himself eternal; therefore,
   The gratitude I feel toward you makes fit
   That while I live, I should declare it here.

And what you tell me of my future, I write—
   And keep it with another text as well,
   Till both are glossed by a lady of good wit

And knowledge, if I reach her. This much still
   I say: so long as conscience is not betrayed,
   I am prepared for Fortune to do her will.   90

My ears find nothing strange in what you have said:
   As Fortune pleases let her wheel be turned,
   And as he must let the peasant turn his spade.'

When he heard these words my master's head inclined
   Toward the right, and looking at me he said,
   'He who has listened well will understand.'

And none the less I continued as I had
   In speech with Ser Brunetto—would he tell
   Which among his companions had enjoyed

Most eminence and fame in life? 'It is well,'   100
   He answered, 'for me to say the names of some
   But nothing of the rest. To name them all

Would demand speaking more words than we have time—
   All clerics and men of letters, all renowned,
   And in the world all stained by this one crime.

Priscian trudges in that unhappy band,
   As does Francesco d'Accorso. And if you crave
   To see such scurf, among them you can find

One whom the Servant of Servants asked to leave
   The Arno for Bacchiglione; and there   110
   He left his body, distended in its nerve

And muscle. And now, although I would say more,
   My speech and walking with you must be brief:
   On the sand, I see new smoke rise, where appear

New souls, with whom I must not be. I live
   In my *Tesoro*—your judgment being won
   For it, I ask no more.' And he went off,

Seeming to me like one of those who run
   Competing for the green cloth in the races

Upon Verona's field—and of them, like one   120

Who gains the victory, not one who loses.

CANTO 33

Pausing in his savage meal, the sinner raised
   His mouth and wiped it clean along the hair
   Left on the head whose back he had laid waste.

Then he began: 'You ask me to endure
   Reliving a grief so desperate, the thought
   Torments my heart even as I prepare

To tell it. But if my words are seeds, with fruit
   Of infamy for this traitor that I gnaw,
   I will both speak and weep within your sight.

I don't know who you are that come here, or how,   10
   But you are surely Florentine to my ear.
   I was Count Ugolino, you must know:

This is Archbishop Ruggieri. You will hear
   Why I am such a neighbour to him as this:
   How, through my trust and his devices, I bore

First being taken, then killed, no need to trace;
   But things which you cannot have heard about—
   The manner of my death, how cruel it was—

I shall describe, and you can tell from that
   If he has wronged me. A slit in the Tower Mew   20
   (Called Hunger's Tower after me, where yet

Others will be closed up) had let me view
   Several moons already, when my bad dream
   Came to me, piercing the future's veil right through:

This man appeared as lord of the hunt; he came
   Chasing a wolf and whelps, on that high slope
   That blocks the Pisans' view of Lucca. With him

His lean hounds ran, well trained and eager; his troop—
   Gualandi, Sismondi, Lanfranchi—had been sent
   To ride in front of him. With no escape,   30

After a short run, father and sons seemed spent;
   I saw their flanks, that sharp fangs seemed to tear.
   I woke before dawn, hearing the complaint

Of my own children, who were with me there,
   Whimpering in their sleep and asking for bread.
   You grieve already, or truly cruel you are,

As you think of what my heart began to dread—
   And if not now, then when do you shed a tear?
   They were awake now, with the hour when food

Was usually brought us drawing near,   40
   And each one apprehensive from his dream.
   And then I heard them nailing shut the door

Into that fearful tower—a pounding that came
   From far below. Hearing that noise, I stared
   Into my children's faces, not speaking to them.

Inside me I was turned to stone, so hard
   I could not weep; the children wept. And my
   Little Anselmo, peering at me, inquired:

"Father, what ails you?" And still I did not cry,
   Nor did I answer, all that day and night   50
   Until the next sun dawned. When one small ray

Found its way into our prison, and I made out
   In their four faces the image of my own,
   I bit my hands for grief; when they saw that,

They thought I did it from my hunger's pain,
   And suddenly rose. "Father: our pain," they said,
   "Will lessen if you eat us—you are the one

Who clothed us in this wretched flesh: we plead
   For you to be the one who strips it away."
   I calmed myself to grieve them less. We stayed   60

Silent through that and then the following day.
   O you hard earth, why didn't you open then?
   When we had reached the fourth day, Gaddo lay

Stretched at my feet where he had fallen down:
   "Father, why don't you help me?" he said, and died.
   And surely as you see me, so one by one

I watched the others fall till all were dead,
   Between the fifth day and the sixth. And I,
   Already going blind, groped over my brood—

Calling to them, though I had watched them die,   70
   For two long days. And then the hunger had more
   Power than even sorrow had over me.'

When he had finished, with a sideways stare
   He gripped the skull again in his teeth, which ground
   Strong as a dog's against the bone he tore.

Ah, Pisa! You shame the peoples of the fair land
   Where *sì* is spoken: slow as your neighbours are
   To punish you, may Gorgona shift its ground,

And Capraia, till those islands make a bar
   To dam the Arno, and drown your populace—   80
   Every soul in you! Though Ugolino bore

The fame of having betrayed your fortresses,
   Still it was wrong in you to so torment
   His helpless children. You Thebes of latter days,

Their youthful ages made them innocent!—
   Uguccione, Brigata, and the two
   My song has named already. On we went,

To where frost roughly swathes a people who,
    Instead of downward, turn their faces up.
    There, weeping keeps them from weeping—for as they do,   90

Grief finds a barrier where the eyes would weep
    But forced back inward, adds to their agonies:
    A crystal visor of prior tears fills the cup

Below the eyebrow with a knot of ice.
    And though, as when a callus has grown numb,
    The cold had sucked all feeling from my face

I sensed a wind, and wondered from where it came:
    'Master, who moves this? Is it not the case
    All vapours are extinguished in this realm?'

'Soon,' he responded, 'you will reach a place   100
    Where your own eyes—beholding what source this blast
    Is poured by from above—will answer this.'

And then one wretch encased in the frozen crust
    Cried out to us, 'O souls so cruel that here,
    Of all the stations, you're assigned the last—

Lift the hard veils away from my face, I implore,
    So that before the weeping freezes again
    I can release a little of this despair

And misery that swell my heart.' Whereon
    I said, 'If you would have me help you, disclose   110
    To me who you are: if I don't help you then,

May I be sent to the bottom of the ice.'
    He answered, 'I am Fra Alberigo, the man
    Of fruit from the evil garden; in this place

I get my payment, date for fig.' 'Oh then,'
    I said to him, 'you are already dead?'
    'I do not know what state my body is in,

Nor how it fares in the world above,' he said.
   'For Ptolomea's privilege is this:
   Down to this place a soul is often conveyed   120

Before it is sent forth by Atropos.
   So that you may more willingly scrape the cowl
   Of tears made hard as glass that coats my face,

Know that as soon as a soul commits betrayal
   The way I did, a devil displaces it
   And governs inside the body until its toll

Of years elapses. Meanwhile, down to this vat
   The soul falls headlong—so it could be true
   That this shade, wintering here behind me, yet

Appears above on earth too: you must know,   130
   If you were sent down only a short time past.
   He is Ser Branca d'Oria; it's years ago

He first arrived here to be thus encased.'
   'Now you deceive me, for I am one who knows
   That Branca d'Oria is not deceased:

He eats and drinks and sleeps and puts on clothes,'
   I told him. And he answered, 'In the ditch
   Ruled by the Malebranche above, that seethes

And bubbles with the lake of clinging pitch,
   The shade of Michel Zanche had not arrived   140
   When this, his killer, had a devil encroach

His body (as did his kinsman, when they contrived
   Together to perform their treachery)
   And take his place in it. Now, as I craved,

Reach out your hand and open my eyes for me.'
   I did not open them—for to be rude
   To such a one as him was courtesy.

Ah Genoese!—to every accustomed good,
   Strangers; with every corruption, amply crowned:
   Why hasn't the world expunged you as it should?   150

For with Romagna's worst spirit I have found
   One of you—already, for deeds he was guilty of,
   Bathed in Cocytus: in soul now underground

Who in body still appears alive, above.

Early *Rime*

Savere e cortesia, ingegno e arte

Wisdom and courtesy, genius and art,
   Beauty and wealth, and true nobility,
   Courage and meekness, and a liberal heart,
   Prowess and excellence, conjoined and singly,
Virtues and graces are that everywhere
   By their sweet power of pleasing conquer Love:
   One than another more of worth may have
   In Love's regard, but each one has a part.
Hence if thou wish, my friend, to make avail
   Thy virtues, whether native or acquired,   10
   Employ them loyally in pleasing Love;
Never oppose his gracious ministry,
   Assured that nothing can defend the man
   Who wages battle wilfully with him.

La dispietata mente, che pur mira

Remembrance, which unpitying turns the view
   Backward to times that are for ever gone,
   On one hand carries war into my heart;
   On th' other hand, the fond desire, which draws
My thoughts to the sweet country I have left,
Oppresses it with all the force of Love:
   Nor do I feel within it strength enough
   And courage to maintain a long defence,
Gentle Madonna, if not helped by you:
   If then you may think fit   10
   Ever to try and save it by your aid,

O now be pleased to send your kind salute,
  By which its virtue may be comforted.

Be pleased, O Lady mine, to fail me not,
  In this the heart's distress which loves you so;
  For succour it expects from you alone.
  The generous master never checks his steed
  When by the servant called who needs relief,
  For his own honour he defends, not him.
  And truly, my heart's grief afflicts me more   20
  When I reflect, Madonna, that your form
  Is there depicted by the hand of Love;
  An argument why you
  Should deem it worthy of the greater care;
  For He, from whom all goodness must be learned,
  Holds us more dear that we his image are.

If you, my sweetest hope, should hesitate,
  And still delay in granting my request,
  Know, that expectance has the limit reached;
  For on the verge of death my powers stand: 30
  And this you cannot doubt, who see me moved
  To seek the very last resource of hope:
  For man should every grievous burthen bear,
  Even the load which presses to the death,
  Rather than prove his greatest friend's true faith,
  Not knowing what may chance.
  And should an evil answer be returned,
  Thing there is not that costs a man so dear;
  For death it hastens and embitters more.

You, lady, are the one whom most I love,   40
  And who the boon most valued can confer,
  And upon whom my hope rests most secure:
  For only to serve you I covet life;
  And what may to your honour best conduce
  I wish and ask; all else to me gives pain:
  'Tis yours to give me what none other dares;
  For 'yes' and 'no' hath Love placed in your hand
  Unfettered; whence my service is my pride.

My confidence in you,
From your humane and noble bearing springs;   50
For he who sees you, by your outward air
Well knows that pity hath her seat within.

Then let your kind salute at last go forth,
  And come into the long expecting heart,
  Whose wishes, gentle lady, you have heard:
But know, that at the entrance there is found
A portal strong, barred by the dart which Love
Hurled on the day when I was made his thrall:
Wherefore admission is denied to all
Except Love's messengers, who have the power   60
To open, by his will who keeps it closed:
Hence in the war I wage,
This aid's arrival might be to my loss,
If unattended by the messengers
Of him, the lord whose pleasure I obey.

My Song, thy journey should be short and swift,
  For well thou knowest how brief will be the time,
  That he who sends thee, if unhelped, can last.

Guido, i' vorrei che tu e Lappo ed io

Guido, I would that Lappo, thou, and I,
  Were carried by some sweet enchantment hence,
  And placed within a bark upon the sea,
  Where wind and wave our bidding should obey;
Where never storm, or other adverse weather,
  To interrupt our course should have the power;
  But wishes ne'er to part should still increase
  By ever living in one mind together.
And might the good enchanter set beside us,
  Our Beatrice, and Vanna, and the lady   10
  Whose place in beauty's list is number thirty;

And there, discoursing ever upon love,
  I trust that each of them would be content,
  As I am confident that we should be.

Per una ghirlandetta

By reason of a garland fair
That once I saw, each single flower
    Now makes me breathe a sigh.
I saw thee, Lady, bear that garland fair,
          Sweetest of flowers that blow,
And over it, as floating in the air
I saw Love's angel hover meek and low,
              And in his song's sweet flow,
              He said, 'Who looks on me
              Will praise my Lord on high.'   10

Should I be haply where a floweret blows,
        A sigh must I suspire,
And say, 'Where'er my gentle lady goes,
Her brow doth bear the flowerets of my Sire:
              But to increase desire,
              My Lady sure will be
              Crownéd by Love's majesty.'

My slender words a tale of flowers have told
              In ballad quaint and new;
And for their brightness they a garment fold,   20
              Not such as others knew.
              Therefore I pray to you,
              That, when one sings it, ye
              Should show it courtesy.

Madonna, quel signor che voi portate

He whom you carry in your eyes, Madonna,
   That sovereign who the mightiest overthrows,
   Sweet confidence inspires
   That I shall find in you compassion's friend.

For where that sovereign fixes his abode,
   And is accompanied by beauty's train,
   All goodness he attracts
   Unto himself, as to the source of power:
   Hence I am ever comforting my hope,
   Which has been harassed in so many storms   10
   It must have suffered wreck,
   If it were not that Love
   Still gives it strength 'gainst all adversity.
   Both by his look, and by the memory
   Of the sweet place, and of the modest flower,
   Which with the glow of youth
   Engarlandeth my mind,
   Thanks, lady, to your gentle courtesy.

De gli occhi de la mia donna si move

Forth from my lady's eyes there streams a light
   So gentle, that wherever she appears
   Things are beheld that may not be described;
   Such their sublimity and nature rare.
And by their beams upon my heart is showered
   Such fear, as makes me tremble and exclaim:
   Here will I never venture to return:
   But soon are all my resolutions lost;
And thither I return, again to fall;
   Giving new courage to the timorous eyes   10
   That had already felt her powerful beams.

Alas! when there arrived, my eyes are closed,
   And the desire which leads them perisheth:
   Hence let my state, O Love, engage thy care.

Ne le man vostre, gentil donna mia

Into thy hands, sweet lady of my soul!
   The spirit that is dying I commend;
   And which departs so sorrowful, that Love
   Views it with pity while dismissing it.
By you to his dominion it was bound
   So firmly, that it since hath had no power
   To call on him, but thus: O mighty lord,
   Whate'er thou wilt of me, thy will is mine.
I know that every wrong displeaseth thee;
   Therefore that death which I have not deserved   10
   Enters my heart with much more bitterness.
O gentle lady, whilst this life remains,
   That I may die in peace, with mind consoled,
   Be pleased to be more bounteous to mine eyes.

Di donne io vidi una gentile schiera

A gentle train of ladies met my view,
   This All Saints' feast, that has but just passed by;
   And one advanced before them as their chief,
   Leading with her, upon her right hand, Love.
She darted from her eyes a dazzling light,
   Which seemed a glorious spirit all of fire:
   And as emboldened on her cheer I gazed,
   I saw depicted there an angel form.
Then with her eyes, benign and soft, she gave

A sweet salute to all who worthy were;   10
  Filling the heart of each with virtuous thoughts.
In heaven, I ween, was born this sovereign lady,
  And came for our salvation to the earth:
  Then blessed is the soul that near her dwells.

Un dì si venne a me Malinconia

Upon a day, came Sorrow in to me,
  Saying, 'I've come to stay with thee a while;'
  And I perceived that she had ushered Bile
And Pain into my house for company.
Wherefore I said, 'Go forth—away with thee!'
  But like a Greek she answered, full of guile,
  And went on arguing in an easy style.
Then, looking, I saw Love come silently,
Habited in black raiment, smooth and new,
  Having a black hat set upon his hair;   10
And certainly the tears he shed were true.
  So that I asked, 'What ails thee, trifler?'
Answering he said: 'A grief to be gone through;
  For our own lady's dying, brother dear.'

The Banquet

Voi che 'ntendendo il terzo ciel movete

Ye who by intellect the third heaven move,
  Give ear unto the reasoning in my heart,
  Which none but you may hear, so strange it seems:
  The heaven that obeys your influence,

Creatures who are all gentleness and love,
Hath drawn me to the state in which I am;
Hence the discourse upon the life I prove,
It seems, should meetly be address'd to you;
Therefore I pray you to attend to me.
I will unfold to you the heart's new cares,   10
How the dejected soul within it weeps;
And how a spirit against her reasoneth,
Which on the beams of your fair star descends.

The joyless heart was wont to be sustain'd
In life by a sweet thought, which often bent
Its flight unto the footstool of your Sire;
Where it beheld a lady glorified,
Of whom so sweetly it discoursed to me,
That the soul said, would I could follow her!
Now appears one which drives the thought away,   20
And rules me with such power, that it makes
The heart to tremble so as to be seen.
A lady this one makes me to regard,
And says, he who would see the bliss of heaven,
Let him intently view this lady's eyes,
Unless the painfulness of sighs he dread.

This rival spirit opposes and destroys
The humble thought, accustom'd to discourse
Of a bright angel who in heaven is crown'd.
The soul so mourns her loss that still she weeps,   30
And says, ah woe is me! how flees away
The pitying thought that was my comforter!
Again, the troubled soul says of mine eyes,
What was the hour this lady look'd on them?
And why believed they not my words of her?
I said, full surely in that lady's eyes
Must dwell the power that such as me destroys;
And it avail'd me not that I foresaw
They should not gaze on her, whence I am dead.

Thou art not dead, but in delusion strayest,   40
Poor soul, who so lamentest thy estate,

Exclaims a little gentle spirit of love;
For this fair lady, who disquiets thee,
Has so transform'd thy life, that thou hast fear
Of her, so spiritless thou art become.
Behold how piteous and how meek she is,
How courteous in her greatness and how sage;
And think to call her mistress evermore:
For thou shalt see, if not by self deceived,
The beauty of such lofty miracles,   50
That thou wilt say, O Love, my sovereign true,
Behold thy handmaid; do as pleaseth thee.

My Song, I do believe that there are few
Who will thy reasoning rightly understand,
To them so hard and dark is thy discourse.
Hence peradventure, if it come to pass
That thou shouldst find thyself with persons who
Appear unskill'd to comprehend thee well,
I pray thee then, my young and well beloved,
Be not discomforted, but say to them,   60
Take note at least how beautiful I am.

Amor, che ne la mente mi ragiona

Love, who discourses to me in my mind
With never-ceasing pleasure of my lady,
Often says things to me concerning her
On which the intellect reflects till lost.
The music of his words so sweetly sounds,
That the attentive soul, which hears and feels,
Exclaims, alas, why have I not the power
To tell what of my lady I do hear?
'Tis sure, that in the first place I must leave,
If I would treat of what I hear of her,   10
That which my reason cannot comprehend,
And of that understood

Great part, from inability of speech.
Hence if my verses shall defective prove,
Which fondly enter on this lady's praise,
The feeble understanding must be blamed,
And our deficient language, wanting power
To paint completely that which Love describes.

The sun, that all this world revolves around,
    Sees not a thing so fair and excellent,   20
    As when he shines upon the part where dwells
    The lady for whom Love commands my song.
    On her all heaven's intelligences gaze;
    And they whom she enamours here below
    Still find her image present to their thoughts,
    When Love calms all emotions into peace.
    With such complacency her Maker views
    His work, that he still showers his gifts on her,
    Beyond our nature's uttermost demand.
    Her pure and spotless soul,   30
    Which from his hand receives this heavenly grace,
    Declares his power in her material frame;
    For in her beauty things are seen so rare,
    That from the eyes of those she shines upon,
    Fly heralds to the heart, with wishes fill'd,
    Which mount into the air and sighs become.

On her the virtue of the Deity
    Descends, as on the angel that beholds him:
    And this if gentle lady disbelieve,
    Let her accompany her, and mark her ways.   40
    Here, when she speaks, an angel boweth down
    From heaven, who joyful testimony bears
    How the high worth of which she is possess'd
    Exceeds the endowments that to us belong.
    The courteous acts which she bestows on all,
    Rival each other in invoking Love,
    With that persuasive voice which makes him hear.
    Of her it may be said
    Fair is in lady what is found in her,
    And most is fair what most resembles her.   50

And truly we may say, her aspect aids
Belief in what appears a miracle,
Hence is our faith confirm'd, and she for this
Hath been created from eternity.

Things in her countenance appear which show
   The ineffable delights of Paradise;
In her sweet smile I say, and in her eyes,
Whither Love brings them as their proper home.
Our intellect they dazzle and subdue,
As the sun's rays o'erpower the feeble sight: 60
And since I may not view them steadfastly,
To say but little I must be content.
Her beauty showers little flames of fire,
With a benignant spirit animate,
Which is creator of all virtuous thought;
And they like thunder crush
The innate vices which make others vile.
The lady then who hears her beauty blamed,
For wanting a deportment calm and meek,
Should view this pattern of humility;   70
'Tis she that humbles every froward heart,
She, whom the mover of the world conceived.

My Song, thy words may seem to contradict
   The language of a sister that thou hast;
For she declares this lady, whom thou makest
So humble, to be scornful and severe:
Thou know'st that heaven is ever clear and bright,
And ever, as regards itself, serene;
But yet our eyes, from causes manifold,
Do sometimes call the sun itself obscure;   80
So when thy sister calls this lady proud,
She views her not according to the truth,
But forms her judgment on appearances:
For fearful was the soul,
And still has fear, so that she seems unkind
Whene'er I see that she observeth me.
Excuse thee thus, my Song, if there be need;
And when thou canst, present thyself to her,

And say, Madonna, if it pleaseth you,
Your praise I will rehearse throughout the world. 90

Le dolci rime d'amor ch' io solia

The pleasant rhymes of Love, that I was wont
   To seek for in my thoughts,
I must forsake; not that I have not hope
   Of a return to them,
But because signs of cruelty and scorn,
   Which in my lady's looks
Are evident, have closed the way against
   My customary strain.
And since it seems to me fit time to wait,
   I will lay down my soft and tender style, 10
That I have held in treating upon Love,
   And of the worth will speak
Which truly gives nobility to man;
   With verse severe and keen
Reproving the opinion false and base
   Of those who hold that of nobility
The principle is wealth.
   And to begin, I here invoke that lord
Whose dwelling-place is in my lady's eyes,
Through whom she is enamour'd of herself. 20

A certain emperor held nobility,
   As it appear'd to him,
To be possession of ancestral wealth
   With generous manners joined:
And there was one of lighter judgment, who
   The saying overthrew;
And took the latter clause away, perchance
   Because he had it not.
Of him the crowd are followers, who affirm
   Those noble who from families are sprung 30

That long have flourish'd in great opulence.
And such the lasting hold
That this so false opinion among us
Has taken, that men call
Him noble who can say I am the son
Or nephew of some certain man of worth,
Though worthless of himself:
But he who looks at truth deems him most vile
To whom the way is shown, and erreth still,
And walks the earth, and yet is as the dead.   40

Who defines man an animated tree,
    Says first what is not true,
    Then adds what is defective to the false;
    But haply sees it not.
    He in like manner who was emperor
    Did in defining err;
    For what is false he first assumed, and then
    Defectively proceeds;
    For riches cannot give nobility,
    As is supposed, nor can they take away,   50
    Since in their very nature they are vile.
    The artist cannot give
    The pictured form unless 'tis in his mind;
    Nor will the upright tower
    Bend to the stream which rolls its wave from far.
    That they imperfect are, and vile, is clear,
    For great howe'er the store,
    They cannot calm, but bring increase of care;
    And hence the mind, which upright is and true,
    Unshaken stands, although they pass away.   60

No man low-born ennobled can become,
    Nor from low sire descend
    A race that noble may be ever deem'd;
    This is by them affirm'd.
    Hence does their reasoning seem to oppose itself;
    Since it maintains that time
    Is requisite to give nobility,
    With time defining it.

It follows from such argument as this,
That all are noble, or that all are base,   70
Or no beginning there has been to man.
But this I cannot grant,
Nor they moreover, if they Christians be.
Wherefore to healthful minds
Their arguments are manifestly vain:
And thus I reprobate their falsity,
And turn from them away;
And now will tell, as it appears to me,
What is nobility, and whence it springs,
And what the signs that mark the noble man.   80

I say, each virtue in its origin
   Springs from a single root;
   Virtue I mean, which happiness bestows
   On man by its good works;
   This is, as Aristotle's *Ethics* say,
   A habit of election,
   Choice of the medium between two extremes;
   And such the words there used.
   I say the nature of nobility
   Ever implies the subject to be good,   90
   As baseness e'er implies the subject bad.
   And virtue such as this
   Gives ever of its goodness proofs to all.
   Since in one predicate
   Two things agree, producing one effect,
   The one must from the other be derived,
   Or each one from a third:
   But if the one equals the other's worth,
   And more, from it that other rather springs:
   Let me on this hypothesis proceed.   100

Nobility must be where virtue is;
   But may be, where 'tis not;
   So heaven is wherever is the sun,
   But not conversely so.
   And we in ladies and in early age
   May see nobility

Evinced in bashfulness and modesty,
Which virtue differ from;
Hence must proceed, as violet from black,
Each several virtue from nobility, 110
Or from the parent root, before explain'd.
Therefore let no one boast,
Saying, nobility is mine by birth;
For they are almost gods,
Who, void of every sin, possess this grace;
For God bestows it only on the soul
Which, in itself, he sees
From imperfection free; so that to few
This seed of happiness is found conjoin'd,
Planted by God in soul aright disposed. 120

The soul that this celestial grace adorns
  In secret hides it not;
  For from the first, when she the body weds,
  She shows it, until death:
Gentle, obedient, and alive to shame,
  Is seen in her first age,
Careful to improve the beauty of her frame
  With all accomplishments:
In youth is temperate and resolute,
Replete with love and praise of courtesy, 130
  Placing in loyalty her sole delight:
  And in declining age
Is prudent, just, and for her bounty known;
  And joys within herself
To listen and discourse for others' good:
Then in the fourth remaining part of life,
  To God is re-espoused,
Contemplating the end which is at hand,
  And blesseth all the seasons that are past.
Reflect now, how the many are deceived! 140

Against the erring multitude, my Song,
  Declaiming, go thy way;
  And where our lady is, when thou shalt be,
  Hide not from her the purport of thy strain;

For truly mayst thou say,
I ever am discoursing of your friend.

From *The Divine Comedy*:

Purgatory

CANTO 5

Now had I left those spirits, and pursued
The steps of my Conductor, when behind
Pointing the finger at me one exclaim'd:

'See how it seems as if the light not shone
From the left hand of him beneath, and he,
As living, seems to be led.' Mine eyes

I at that sound reverting, saw them gaze
Through wonder first at me, and then at me
And the light broken underneath, by turns.

  'Why are thy thoughts thus riveted,' my guide   10
Exclaim'd, 'that thou hast slack'd thy pace? or how
Imports it thee, what thing is whisper'd here?

Come after me, and to their babblings leave
The crowd. Be as a tower, that, firmly set,
Shakes not its top for any blast that blows!

He, in whose bosom thought on thought shoots out,
Still of his aim is wide, in that the one
Sicklies and wastes to nought the other's strength.'

  What other could I answer save 'I come'?
I said it, somewhat with that colour ting'd   20
Which ofttimes pardon meriteth for man.

  Meanwhile traverse along the hill there came,
A little way before us, some who sang
The 'Miserere' in responsive strains.

When they perceiv'd that through my body I
Gave way not for the rays to pass, their song
Strait to a long and hoarse exclaim they chang'd;

And two of them, in guise of messengers,
Ran on to meet us, and inquiring ask'd:
'Of your condition we would gladly learn.'   30

  To them my guide. 'Ye may return, and bear
Tidings to them who sent you, that his frame
Is real flesh. If, as I deem, to view

His shade they paus'd, enough is answer'd them.
Him let them honour, they may prize him well.'
  Ne'er saw I fiery vapours with such speed

Cut through the serene air at fall of night,
Nor August's clouds athwart the setting sun,
That upward these did not in shorter space

Return; and, there arriving, with the rest   40
Wheel back on us, as with loose rein a troop.
  'Many,' exclaim'd the bard, 'are these, who throng

Around us: to petition thee they come.
Go therefore on, and listen as thou go'st.'
  'O spirit! who go'st on to blessedness

With the same limbs, that clad thee at thy birth,'
Shouting they came, 'a little rest thy step.
Look if thou any one amongst our tribe

Hast e'er beheld, that tidings of him there
Thou mayst report. Ah, wherefore go'st thou on?   50
Ah wherefore tarriest thou not? We all

By violence died, and to our latest hour
Were sinners, but then warn'd by light from heav'n,
So that, repenting and forgiving, we

Did issue out of life at peace with God,
Who with desire to see him fills our heart.'
   Then I: 'The visages of all I scan

Yet none of ye remember. But if aught,
That I can do, may please you, gentle spirits!
Speak; and I will perform it, by that peace,   60

Which on the steps of guide so excellent
Following from world to world intent I seek.'
   In answer he began: 'None here distrusts

Thy kindness, though not promis'd with an oath;
So as the will fail not for want of power.
Whence I, who sole before the others speak,

Entreat thee, if thou ever see that land,
Which lies between Romagna and the realm
Of Charles, that of thy courtesy thou pray

Those who inhabit Fano, that for me   70
Their adorations duly be put up,
By which I may purge off my grievous sins.

From thence I came. But the deep passages,
Whence issued out the blood wherein I dwelt,
Upon my bosom in Antenor's land

Were made, where to be more secure I thought.
The author of the deed was Este's prince,
Who, more than right could warrant, with his wrath

Pursued me. Had I towards Mira fled,
When overta'en at Oriaco, still   80
Might I have breath'd. But to the marsh I sped,

And in the mire and rushes tangled there
Fell, and beheld my life-blood float the plain.'
   Then said another: 'Ah! so may the wish,

That takes thee o'er the mountain, be fulfill'd,
As thou shalt graciously give aid to mine.
Of Montefeltro I; Buonconte I:

Giovanna nor none else have care for me,
Sorrowing with these I therefore go.' I thus:
'From Campaldino's field what force or chance   90

Drew thee, that ne'er thy sepulture was known?'
   'Oh!' answer'd he, 'at Casentino's foot
A stream there courseth, nam'd Archiano, sprung

In Apennine above the Hermit's seat.
E'en where its name is cancel'd, there came I,
Pierc'd in the heart, fleeing away on foot,

And bloodying the plain. Here sight and speech
Fail'd me, and finishing with Mary's name
I fell, and tenantless my flesh remain'd.

I will report the truth; which thou again   100
Tell to the living. Me God's angel took,
Whilst he of hell exclaim'd: "O thou from heav'n!

"Say wherefore has thou robb'd me? Thou of him
"Th' eternal portion bear'st with thee away
"For one poor tear that he deprives me of.

"But of the other, other rule I make."
   'Thou knowst how in the atmosphere collects
That vapour dank, returning into water,

Soon as it mounts where cold condenses it.
That evil will, which in his intellect   110
Still follows evil, came, and rais'd the wind

And smoky mist, by virtue of the power
Giv'n by his nature. Thence the valley, soon
As day was spent, he cover'd o'er with cloud

From Pratomagno to the mountain range,
And stretch'd the sky above, so that the air
Impregnate chang'd to water. Fell the rain,

And to the fosses came all that the land
Contain'd not; and, as mightiest streams are wont,
To the great river with such headlong sweep   120

Rush'd, that nought stay'd its course. My stiffen'd frame
Laid at his mouth the fell Archiano found,
And dash'd it into Arno, from my breast

Loos'ning the cross, that of myself I made
When overcome with pain. He hurl'd me on.
Along the banks and bottom of his course;

Then in his muddy spoils encircling wrapt.'
   'Ah! when thou to the world shalt be return'd,
And rested after thy long road,' so spake

Next the third spirit; 'then remember me.   130
I once was Pia. Sienna gave me life,
Maremma took it from me. That he knows,

Who me with jewell'd ring had first espous'd.'

CANTO 6

When from their game of dice men separate,
He, who hath lost, remains in sadness fix'd,
Revolving in his mind, what luckless throws

He cast: but meanwhile all the company
Go with the other; one before him runs,
And one behind his mantle twitches, one

Fast by his side bids him remember him.
He stoops not; and each one, to whom his hand
Is stretch'd, well knows he bids him stand aside;

And thus he from the press defends himself.   10
E'en such was I in that close-crowding throng;
And turning so my face around to all,

And promising, I 'scap'd from it with pains.
   Here of Arezzo him I saw, who fell
By Ghino's cruel arm; and him beside,

Who in his chase was swallow'd by the stream.
Here Frederick Novello, with his hand
Stretch'd forth, entreated; and of Pisa he,

Who put the good Marzuco to such proof
Of constancy. Count Orso I beheld;   20
And from its frame a soul dismiss'd for spite

And envy, as it said, but for no crime:
I speak of Peter de la Brosse; and here,
While she yet lives, that Lady of Brabant

Let her beware; lest for so false a deed
She herd with worse than these. When I was freed
From all those spirits, who pray'd for others' prayers

To hasten on their state of blessedness;
Strait I begin: 'O thou, my luminary!
It seems expressly in thy text denied,   30

That heaven's supreme decree can ever bend
To supplication; yet with this design
Do these entreat. Can then their hope be vain,

Or is thy saying not to me reveal'd?'
   He thus to me: 'Both what I write is plain,
And these deceiv'd not in their hope, if well

They mind consider, that the sacred height
Of judgment doth not stoop, because love's flame
In a short moment all fulfils, which he

Who sojourns here, in right should satisfy.   40
Besides, when I this point concluded thus,
By praying no defect could be supplied;

Because the pray'r had none access to God.
Yet in this deep suspicion rest thou not
Contented, unless she assure thee so,

Who betwixt truth and mind infuses light.
I know not if thou take me right; I mean
Beatrice. Her thou shalt behold above,

Upon this mountain's crown, fair seat of joy.'
    Then I: 'Sir! let us mend our speed; for now   50
I tire not as before: and lo! the hill

Stretches its shadow far.' He answer'd thus:
'Our progress with this day shall be as much
As we may now dispatch; but otherwise

Than thou supposest is the truth. For there
Thou canst not be, ere thou once more behold
Him back returning, who behind the steep

Is now so hidden, that as erst his beam
Thou dost not break. But lo! a spirit there
Stands solitary, and toward us looks: 60

It will instruct us in the speediest way.'
    We soon approach'd it. O thou Lombard spirit!
How didst thou stand, in high abstracted mood,

Scarce moving with slow dignity thine eyes!
It spoke not aught, but let us onward pass,
Eyeing us as a lion on his watch.

But Virgil with entreaty mild advanc'd,
Requesting it to show the best ascent.
It answer to his question none return'd,

But of our country and our kind of life   70
Demanded. When my courteous guide began,
'Mantua,' the solitary shadow quick

Rose tow'rds us from the place in which it stood,
And cry'd, 'Mantuan! I am thy countryman
Sordello.' Each the other then embrac'd.

    Ah slavish Italy! thou inn of grief,
Vessel without a pilot in loud storm,
Lady no longer of fair provinces,

But brothel-house impure! this gentle spirit,
Ev'n from the pleasant sound of his dear land   80
Was prompt to greet a fellow citizen

With such glad cheer; while now thy living ones
In thee abide not without war; and one
Malicious gnaws another, ay of those

Whom the same wall and the same moat contains.
Seek, wretched one! around thy sea-coasts wide;
Then homeward to thy bosom turn, and mark

If any part of thee sweet peace enjoy.
What boots it, that thy reins Justinian's hand
Refitted, if thy saddle be unpress'd?   90

Nought doth he now but aggravate thy shame.
Ah people! thou obedient still shouldst live,
And in the saddle let thy Caesar sit,

If well thou marked'st that which God commands.
    Look how that beast to felness hath relaps'd
From having lost correction of the spur,

Since to the bridle thou hast set thine hand,
O German Albert who abandon'st her,
That is grown savage and unmanageable,

When thou should'st clasp her flanks with forked heels.   100
Just judgment from the stars fall on thy blood!
And be it strange and manifest to all!

Such as may strike thy successor with dread!
For that thy sire and thou have suffer'd thus,
Through greediness of yonder realms detain'd,

The garden of the empire to run waste.
Come see the Capulets and Montagues,
The Philippeschi and Monaldi! man

Who car'st for nought! those sunk in grief, and these
With dire suspicion rack'd. Come, cruel one!   110
Come and behold th' oppression of the nobles,

And mark their injuries: and thou mayst see,
What safety Santafiore can supply.
Come and behold thy Rome, who calls on thee,

Desolate widow! day and night with moans:
'My Caesar, why dost thou desert my side?'
Come and behold what love among thy people:

And if no pity touches thee for us,
Come, and blush for thine own report. For me,
If it be lawful, O Almighty Power,   120

Who wast in earth for our sakes crucified!
Are thy just eyes turn'd elsewhere? or is this
A preparation in the wond'rous depth

Of thy sage counsel made, for some good end,
Entirely from our reach of thought cut off?
So are th' Italian cities all o'erthrong'd

With tyrants, and a great Marcellus made
Of every petty factious villager.
  My Florence! thou mayst well remain unmov'd

At this digression, which affects not thee: 130
Thanks to thy people, who so wisely speed.
Many have justice in their heart, that long

Waiteth for counsel to direct the bow,
Or ere it dart unto its aim: but thine
Have it on their lip's edge. Many refuse

To bear the common burdens: readier thine
Answer uncall'd, and cry, 'Behold I stoop!'
  Make thyself glad, for thou hast reason now,

Thou wealthy! thou at peace! thou wisdom-fraught!
Facts best will witness if I speak the truth.   140
Athens and Lacedæmon, who of old

Enacted laws, for civil arts renown'd,
Made little progress in improving life
Tow'rds thee, who usest such nice subtlety,

That to the middle of November scarce
Reaches the thread thou in October weav'st.
How many times, within thy memory,

Customs, and laws, and coins, and offices
Have been by thee renew'd, and people chang'd!
  If thou rememberst well and can'st see clear,   150

Thou wilt perceive thyself like a sick wretch,
Who finds no rest upon her down, but oft
Shifting her side, short respite seeks from pain.

CANTO 26

While singly thus along the rim we walk'd,
Oft the good master warn'd me: 'Look thou well.
Avail it that I caution thee.' The sun

Now all the western clime irradiate chang'd
From azure tint to white; and, as I pass'd,
My passing shadow made the umber'd flame

Burn ruddier. At so strange a sight I mark'd
That many a spirit marvel'd on his way.
     This bred occasion first to speak of me.

'He seems,' said they, 'no insubstantial frame:'   10
Then to obtain what certainty they might,
Stretch'd towards me, careful not to overpass

The burning pale. 'O thou, who followest
The others, haply not more slow than they,
But mov'd by rev'rence, answer me, who burn

In thirst and fire: nor I alone, but these
All for thine answer do more thirst, than doth
Indian or Æthiop for the cooling stream.

Tell us, how it is that thou mak'st thyself
A wall against the sun, as thou not yet   20
Into th' inextricable toils of death

Hadst enter'd?' Thus spake one; and I had straight
Declar'd me, if attention had not turn'd
To new appearance. Meeting these, there came,

Midway the burning path, a crowd, on whom
Earnestly gazing, from each part I view
The shadows all press forward, sev'rally

Each snatch a hasty kiss, and then away.
E'en so the emmets, 'mid their dusky troops,
Peer closely one at other, to spy out   30

Their mutual road perchance, and how they thrive.
    That friendly greeting parted, ere dispatch
Of the first onward step, from either tribe

Loud clamour rises: those, who newly come,
Shout 'Sodom and Gomorrah!' these, 'The cow
Pasiphae enter'd, that the beast she woo'd

Might rush unto her luxury.' Then as cranes,
That part towards the Riphæan mountains fly,
Part towards the Lybic sands, these to avoid

The ice, and those the sun; so hasteth off   40
One crowd, advances th' other; and resume
Their first song weeping, and their several shout.

    Again drew near my side the very same,
Who had erewhile besought me, and their looks
Mark'd eagerness to listen. I, who twice

Their will had noted, spake: 'O spirits secure,
Whene'er the time may be, of peaceful end!
My limbs, nor crude, nor in mature old age,

Have I left yonder: here they bear me, fed   50
With blood, and sinew-strung. That I no more
May live in blindness, hence I tend aloft.

There is a dame on high, who wins for us
This grace, by which my mortal through your realm
I bear. But may your utmost wish soon meet

Such full fruition, that the orb of heaven,
Fullest of love, and of most ample space,
Receive you, as ye tell (upon my page

Henceforth to stand recorded) who ye are,
And what this multitude, that at your backs
Have past behind us.' As one, mountain-bred,   60

Rugged and clownish, if some city's walls
He chance to enter, round him stares agape,
Confounded and struck dumb; e'en such appear'd

Each spirit. But when rid of that amaze,
(Not long the inmate of a noble heart)
He, who before had question'd, thus resum'd:

'O blessed, who, for death preparing, tak'st
Experience of our limits, in thy bark!
Their crime, who not with us proceed was that,

For which, as he did triumph, Cæsar heard   70
The shout of "queen," to taunt him. Hence their cry
Of "Sodom," as they parted, to rebuke

Themselves, and aid the burning by their shame.
Our sinning was Hermaphrodite: but we,
Because the law of human kind we broke,

Following like beasts our vile concupiscence,
Hence parting from them, to our own disgrace
Record the name of her, by whom the beast

In bestial tire was acted. Now our deeds
Thou know'st, and how we sinn'd. If thou by name   80
Wouldst haply know us, time permits not now

To tell so much, nor can I. Of myself
Learn what thou wishest. Guinicelli I,
Who having truly sorrow'd ere my last,

Already cleanse me.' With such pious joy,
As the two sons upon their mother gaz'd
From sad Lycurgus rescu'd, such my joy

(Save that I more represt it) when I heard
From his own lips the name of him pronounc'd,
Who was a father to me, and to those   90

My betters, who have ever us'd the sweet
And pleasant rhymes of love. So nought I heard
Nor spake, but long time thoughtfully I went,

Gazing on him; and, only for the fire,
Approach'd not nearer. When my eyes were fed
By looking on him, with such solemn pledge,

As forces credence, I devoted me
Unto his service wholly. In reply
He thus bespake me: 'What from thee I hear

Is grav'd so deeply on my mind, the waves   100
Of Lethe shall not wash it off, nor make
A whit less lively. But as now thy oath

Has seal'd the truth, declare what cause impels
That love, which both thy looks and speech bewray.'
    'Those dulcet lays;' I answer'd, 'which, as long

As of our tongue the beauty does not fade,
Shall make us love the very ink that trac'd them.'
    'Brother!' he cried, and pointed at a shade

Before him, 'there is one, whose mother speech
Doth owe to him a fairer ornament.   110
He in love ditties and the tales of prose

Without a rival stands, and lets the fools
Talk on, who think the songster of Limoges
O'ertops him. Rumour and the popular voice

They look to more than truth, and so confirm
Opinion, ere by art or reason taught.
Thus many of the elder time cried up

Guittone, giving him the prize, till truth
By strength of numbers vanquish'd. If thou own
So ample privilege, as to have gain'd   120

Free entrance to the cloister, whereof Christ
Is Abbot of the college, say to him
One paternoster for me, far as needs

For dwellers in this world, where power to sin
No longer tempts us.' Haply to make way
For one, that follow'd next, when that was said,

He vanish'd through the fire, as through the wave
A fish, that glances diving to the deep.
　　I, to the spirit he had shown me, drew

A little onward, and besought his name, 130
For which my heart, I said, kept gracious room.
He frankly thus began: 'Thy courtesy

So wins on me, I have nor power nor will
To hide me. I am Arnault; and with songs,
Sorely waymenting for my folly past,

Thorough this ford of fire I wade, and see
The day, I hope for, smiling in my view.
I pray ye by the worth that guides ye up

Unto the summit of the scale, in time
Remember ye my suff'rings.' With such words 140
He disappear'd in the refining flame.

Later *Rime*

Voi che savete ragionar d' Amore

Ye who are able to discourse of Love,
    Attend I pray and hear my piteous song,
    Which tells of a disdainful lady's scorn,
    Who by her worth hath robbed me of my heart.

Such is her scorn of all who look on her
    That she compels the eyes to bow through fear;
    For round her own there plays unceasingly
    A portraiture of every cruelty;
    Yet the sweet image do they bear within
    Which prompts the gentle soul to say: Be kind!   10
    And has such virtue when it is beheld,
    That it draws forth the sighs from every heart.

She seems to say, Ne'er will I gracious be
    To any one shall look upon mine eyes;
    For I within them bear that gentle Lord
    Who makes me feel the virtue of his darts.
    And truly I believe she guards them thus
    To view them at her pleasure and alone,
    As looks a modest lady in her mirror,
    Desirous that when seen she may be honoured.   20

No hope have I that she will ever deign
    From pity to bestow a glance on man,
    So cruel in her beauty is this lady,
    She who feels Love a dweller in her eyes.
    But let her hide and guard him as she will,
    That for a while I may not see such bliss,
    Yet my desires at last shall have the power
    To conquer the disdain I bear from Love.

Parole mie che per lo mondo siete

Ye words of mine, whose voice the world doth fill,
    Who had your birth when first my thoughts began
    To speak of her for whom astray I ran;
'Ye, who the third heaven move, by force of will,'
Knowing her well, to her your course fulfil,
    So wailing that she may our sorrows scan:
    Say to her, 'We are thine, nor think we can
Present ourselves henceforth more numerous still.'

Stay not with her; for Love is not found there,
    But take your way around in sad array,   10
Like your own sisters in the days that were.
And when ye find a lady kind and fair,
    Right humbly at her feet your tribute lay,
And say, 'To thee we gifts of honour bear.'

O dolci rime che parlando andate

Sweet rhymes, whose theme is still the gentle lady
   Who on all other ladies sheddeth honour,
   To you will come, perchance ere now is come,
   One whom you hail, and say: This is our brother.
O by that lord who every lady's breast
   Enamours, I conjure you turn your ear
   From his discourse, for in his mind there dwells
   No sentiment which is the friend of truth.
And should you by his language have been moved
   To journey to the lady whom you serve,   10
   Stay not your course; but to her presence haste,
And say to her: Our errand is, Madonna,
   To recommend one who in grief exclaims:
   Ah me! Where is the desire of mine eyes?

Due donne in cima de la mente mia

Two ladies, to the summit of my mind,
    Are come to hold discourse concerning love:
    Virtue and courtesy adorn the one,
    With modesty and prudence in her train;
Beauty, and lively elegance, the other;
    And gentleness combines to do her honour:
    And I, by favour of my gracious lord,
    Stand at the footstool of their sovereignty.
Beauty and virtue both address the mind,
    And question if a heart can truly serve   10
    Two ladies, and with perfect love to each:
The fountain of pure eloquence replies,
    That Beauty may be loved for her delights,
    And Virtue may be loved for lofty deeds

I' mi son pargoletta bella e nova

Ladies, behold a maiden fair and young;
    To you I come, to show you in myself
    The beauties of the place where I have been.

In heaven I dwelt, and thither shall return,
    To impart delight to others with my beams:
    And he who sees me and is not enamoured,
    Shall never have intelligence of love;
    For every pleasing gift was freely given,
    When Nature sought the grant of me from Him
    Who willed that I should bear you company.   10

Each planet showers down upon mine eyes
    Most bounteously its virtue and its light:
    Beauties are mine the world hath never seen,
    For I obtained them in the realms above;

And ever must their nature rest unknown,
Unless to the intelligence of Him
In whom Love dwells to give to others bliss.

These words were written on the gentle brow
Of a fair angel who appeared to us;
Whence I, to save myself, gazed full on her,   20
And hazarded the losing of my life;
For so severe a wound I then received
From one whom I beheld within her eyes,
That ever since I weep, nor peace have known.

Io sento sì d'Amor la gran posanza

I feel the mighty power of Love so great
That I can not endure
Its suffering long; whence I am sorely grieved;
For he is ever growing in his strength,
And I feel mine decay;
So that each hour I am weaker than before.
I ask not Love to grant more than I wish,
For should he grant all that the will requires,
The virtue which from nature I derive
Could bear it not, for it is limited:
And this it is of which my heart complains,   10
That power corresponds not to desire.
But if from good desire reward should spring,
I claim it, in a grant of longer life,
From those fair eyes, whose splendour, sweetly mild,
Brings comfort when I feel Love's influence.

The rays proceeding from those beauteous eyes
Pierce mine of her enamoured,
And sweets impart where bitterness I feel;
And journey onwards, like to travellers
Who erst have passed that way;   20

Remembering the place where Love they left,
When through the eyes they led him to my heart.
Thus their return confers a boon on me;
And when they hide themselves they do her wrong
Whose votary I am, with love so true,
That life I only prize for serving her;
And all my thoughts, which spring from Love alone,
Press forward to her service as their goal.
So strong my zeal to labour for her good,
That could I think 'twere gained by leaving her,   30
Light were the task, though certain were my death.

O true must be the love which captivates,
   And strong must be the chain,
   Since I would do for it what I aver:
For love exists not of an equal weight
   To that which pleasure finds
   In death, from serving of another well.
And in this will I was confirmed, as soon
As birth was given to the strong desire
I feel, through virtue of the pleasing traits   40
Of that fair face, where all that's fair is found.
Servant I am, and, when I think of whom,
And what she is, perfect content is mine:
For man may serve her well against her will;
And though her youth may rob me of reward,
Hope shows a time when she will be more just;
   Provided life defend itself so long.

When on a sweet desire I meditate,
   Born of the grand desire
   Which all my energies to virtue prompts,   50
I seem rewarded far above desert;
   And further still, I seem
   Wrongly the name of servant to retain:
For service is converted to good-will,
When viewed with pleasure by a master kind;
But since to rigid truth I would adhere,
   'Tis fit that such desire be service deemed;
   For all my efforts made to labour well,

Are less directed to my private good,
Than that of her, who holds me in her power.   60
I labour that her worth may more be prized,
And am entirely hers. It is my pride
That Love hath made me worthy of such honour.

No power but that of Love could render me
   Deserving to be made
   Subject of her, who never is enamoured;
   But, as a lady unconcerned, regards
   The mind inspired with love,
   That cannot pass without her one short hour:
   I have not seen her yet so many times   70
   That beauty which is new I have not found;
   Whence love within me gains increasing strength
   From every new addition to the pleasure;
   And hence my state remains unchanged, so long
   As Love accustoms me by turns to feel
   One bitter suffering, and one sweet delight,
   Dependent on that time of frequent pain,
   Which lasts from when I lose the sight of her,
   Until the moment when it is regained.

My beauteous Song, if thou resemblest me,   80
   Thou wilt show less disdain,
   Than goodness such as thine might well become;
   Hence I beseech thee subtilise thy skill,
   My sweet and lovely one,
   In choosing mode or way may suit thy need
   If cavalier invite thee, or retain,
   Before thou with his pleasure dost comply,
   Spy whether thou canst make him of thy sect;
   And if thou canst not, leave him with all speed;
   For with the good the good are ever found: 90
   But oft it happens, that with one we are thrown
   In company, who is unjustly blamed,
   By ill report spread by another's tongue.
   The wicked shun, though famed for wit or skill,
   For it were never wise to sort with them.

My Song, before thou elsewhere take thy way,
    Go to the three least guilty of our city:
    Salute the two, the other strive to win,
    And from an evil sect to draw away:
    Tell him, the good ne'er war against the good;   100
    But rather strive the wicked to subdue;
    Tell him, that he who through the fear of shame
    From folly flies not, is a fool indeed;
    But he may fear who is of vice afraid,
    For shunning one he finds the other's cure.

Io son venuto al punto de la rota

The circling year's cold point I have attained,
    When the horizon gives the sun repose,
    And in the east brings forth the heavenly twins.
    The star of Love remains removed from view,
    Hid by the lucid ray, across it thrown,
    So widely as to form for it a veil:
    The planet also which gives strength to frost
    Moves full disclosed through the capacious arch,
    In which each of the seven cast little shade:
    And yet no thought of Love,   10
    With which I am loaded, ever quits my mind,
    That harder is than agate to retain
    The image of a lady formed of stone.

In Ethiopia's sands the pilgrim wind
    Arises and the lurid air disturbs,
    That burns beneath the scorching solar ray;
    Then, the sea passing, draws from it a mist
    So thick, that if no other wind disturb,
    It covers and shuts up this hemisphere;
    And then dissolves, and falls in whitened flakes   20
    Of chilling snow, or showers of noisome rain,
    Whence saddened is the air, and nature mourns.

Yet Love, who all his nets
Withdraws to heaven, as the tempest swells,
Never abandons me, beauty so great
Adorns this cruel lady whom I serve.

Each bird that seeks the genial heat hath fled
From Europe's lands, in whose extensive bounds
The seven frosty stars are never lost;
The voices of the rest are silent all,   30
To sound no more till verdant spring's return;
Unless it be that grief calls forth their plaints;
And every animal by nature gay
Is liberated from the thrall of Love,
Their spirit being deadened by the cold;
And mine with love burns more:
For never am I robbed of the sweet thoughts
Which are not given me by the season's change,
But by a lady in youth's tender spring.

The leaves have passed the fated term, prescribed   40
When Aries by his influence drew them forth
To decorate the world; the grass is dead,
And every verdant bough from us is hidden,
Save in the pine, the laurel, or the fir,
Or other plant by nature ever green.
The season too is harsh, and so severe,
That all the pretty flowerets of the plain
Are killed, unable to endure the frost;
Yet is the amorous thorn
Fixed in my heart, nor Love can it withdraw;   50
For firm is my resolve to hold it there,
Long as I live, though life should never end.

The veins pour forth the watery streams which smoke
From vapours that earth holds within her womb,
Sending them up aloft from the abyss,
Whence glad I found a road to cheerful day
Now to a river changed, and such shall be,
Long as stern winter's rude assault shall last.
Enamelled is the surface of the earth,

And the dead pool converted into glass, 60
Through cold which closes every outward pore:
Yet I still wage my war,
Nor backward have recoiled a single step,
Nor will recoil; for if the pain be sweet,
All other sweets must be surpassed by death.

My Song, say what will be my fate, in days
Far different and sweet, when Love shall shower
His blessings on the earth from every heaven;
Since even amid these frosts
Love is in me alone, nor elsewhere found? 70
My fate will be that of a man of stone,
If stone shall be this tender maiden's heart.

Al poco giorno e al gran cerchio d'ombra

To the dim light and the large circle of shade
I have clomb, and to the whitening of the hills,
There where we see no colour in the grass,
Nathless my longing loses not its green,
It has so taken root in the hard stone
Which talks and hears as though it were a lady.

Utterly frozen is this youthful lady,
Even as the snow that lies within the shade;
For she is no more moved than is the stone
By the sweet season which makes warm the hills 10
And alters them afresh from white to green,
Covering their sides again with flowers and grass.

When on her hair she sets a crown of grass
The thought has no more room for other lady;
Because she weaves the yellow with the green
So well that Love sits down there in the shade,—

Love who has shut me in among low hills
Faster than between walls of granite-stone.

She is more bright than is a precious stone;
The wound she gives may not be healed with grass   20
I therefore have fled far o'er plains and hills
For refuge from so dangerous a lady;
But from her sunshine nothing can give shade,—
Not any hill nor wall, nor summer-green.

A while ago, I saw her dressed in green,—
So fair, she might have wakened in a stone
This love which I do feel even for her shade;
And therefore, as one woos a graceful lady,
I wooed her in a field that was all grass,
Girdled about with very lofty hills.   30

Yet shall the streams turn back and climb the hills
Before Love's flame in this damp wood and green
Burn, as it burns within a youthful lady,
For my sake, who would sleep away in stone
My life, or feed like beasts upon the grass,
Only to see her garments cast a shade.

How dark soe'er the hills throw out their shade,
Under her summer-green the beautiful lady
Covers it, like a stone covered in grass.

Così nel mio parlar voglio esser aspro

Severe shall be my speech, as in her deeds
   Is she, the rock so beautiful and cold,
   Who every hour acquires
   More hardness and a nature more unkind:
   And clothes her person, too, in adamant,
   So that by strength of armour, or retreat,
   No quiver sends a dart

Can ever reach a part of her exposed;
And she still wounds; nor space nor coat of mail
Can man protect, to escape her mortal blows,   10
Which fly as they had wings,
And him o'ertake, and all his armour rend;
Whence skill or might avails me not 'gainst her.

No shield of mine I find but she can break,
   No place that can conceal me from her view;
   Yet as the flower crowns
   The stem, so she the summit of my mind.
   Regardless of my pain she seems, and moved
   No more than ship unlifted by the wave.
   The weight which sinks me down   20
   Is such as verse unequal were to tell:
   Alas! thou pitiless, tormenting file,
   Which silently art shortening my life,
   Why fear'st thou not as much,
   By piecemeal, thus to wear my heart,
   As I to tell the world whence springs thy power?

My heart more trembles when I think of her
   In place where I may draw another's eye,
   Through terror lest my thought
   Should glimmer through the veil, and be discerned,   30
   Than when I think of death, who every sense
   Already with the teeth of Love devours.
   The thought on which I muse
   Strips bare my energy, and slacks its work.
   By Love I am stricken down, who o'er me stands,
   Wielding the sword with which he Dido slew.
   Suppliant I call on him
   Imploring mercy in a humble prayer:
   And he seems fixed all mercy to deny.

From time to time this cruel victor lifts   40
   His hand, in threats to take my feeble life;
   Thrown down and stretched on earth
   He holds me, wearied out with struggling:
   Then cries of anguish rise within my mind,

And the red blood, dispersed throughout the veins,
  Runs swift toward the heart,
  Which calls it, leaving me all pale and wan.
  On the left side, he strikes me with such force,
  That with the agony the heart rebounds.
  I then say: should he lift   50
  His hand again, Death's arms will me enfold
  Ere that the blow shall have descended down.

O could I see him cleave the heart in twain
  Of her, the cruel one, who mangles mine;
  Death then would not appal,
  To whom I hasten through her beauty's charm:
  For this assassin, who both robs and kills,
  Wrongs me alike in sunshine and in shade.
  Alas! why cries she not
  For me, as I for her, engulfed in fire?   60
  For quick would I exclaim: Your help is here;
  And anxious to assist, would do like him
  Who in the flaxen locks,
  Which Love for my destruction crisps and gilds,
  Would fix the hand; and then my bliss were full.

When once those golden tresses I had seized,
  Which have to me as scourges been and goads,
  Though grasped before the dawn,
  Them would I hold at vespers and each bell;
  Nor piteous nor courteous would I be,   70
  But like the bear in sportive mood would play:
  And should Love punish me,
  I then would be a thousand fold avenged:
  And on those beauteous eyes, whence fly the sparks
  That evermore inflame my wounded heart,
  Close would I fix my gaze,
  To be revenged for her avoiding me;
  And then would peace restore to her, with love.

My Song, unto the lady straight repair,
  By whom my heart is wounded, and who steals   80
  From me my chief delight;

And pierce her with an arrow through the heart;
For bright the honour by revenge acquired.

Tre donne intorno al cor mi son venute

Three ladies have retreated to my heart,
    And at the portal sit,
    Where Love resides within,
Who in his sovereignty commands my life.
So great their beauty, and their virtue such,
    That he, the mighty lord,
    Whose seat is in my heart,
Can scarcely find fit terms to speak of them.
Each one seems melancholy and in fear
    Like an unhappy exile faint and weary,   10
    Whom all the world forsakes,
And nobleness and virtue nought avail.
    In days of old they were
    (As report tells of them) mankind's delight;
Now are they hated and contemned by all.
    These ladies, thus forlorn,
    Are come as to the mansion of a friend;
For well they know that he I name dwells there.

In many a piteous note one vents her grief,
    And on her hand reclines,   20
    Like a dissevered rose;
The naked arm, the pillar of her woe,
Feels the bright gem, which from the cheek drops down:
    The other hand conceals
    The face bedewed with tears;
Unshod, unzoned, she still appears a lady.
Soon as the tattered gown revealed to Love
    Her form in part, of which to speak were wrong,
    Pity he felt and wrath,
And questions asked of her and of her grief.   30

O thou, the staff of few,
She said, in voice oft broken by her sighs,
The claim of kindred sends us here to thee.
I, who do sorrow most,
Am Rectitude, the sister of thy mother;
How poor, thou seest by these my robes and zone.

When she had made herself thus clearly known,
  My sovereign was seized
  With grief and shame, and asked,
Who were the other two who were with her.   40
And she, who was so prone to melt in tears.
  Soon as she heard his words,
  Burned with increase of woe,
Saying: Now grievest thou not to see these eyes?
Then thus began: The Nile, as well thou knowest,
  Springs forth a little river at its source,
  In land where heaven's great light
Deprives the earth of every willow's leaf:
  Beside that virgin wave,
I brought forth her who here is at my side,   50
  And with her flaxen tresses dries the tear:
  And she, my fair offspring,
Herself admiring in the fountain pure
Brought forth this other, more removed from me.

Love paused awhile, his speech being checked by sighs;
  And then, with softened eyes
  Which playful were at first,
Saluted his unhappy relatives.
He after took a dart of either kind,
  And said: Look up, be cheered;   60
  Behold the arms I need,
Now soiled and dull you see, from want of use.
  Bounty and Temperance, and the others who
  Are daughters of our blood, in beggary rove.
  But though this be an ill,
Let the eyes weep for it, and lips lament
  Of men, whom it concerns,
And are exposed to influence of such skies;

Not we, who are of the eternal rock;
For though sore wounded now,   70
Yet still shall we endure, and yet shall find
A race by whom this dart shall shine again.

And I, who hear the speech divine, and see
   How exiles great as these
   Are grieved and comforted,
Henceforth my banishment an honour deem:
And though a judgment, or the force of fate,
   Wills that this fickle world should change
   The flowers white to black,
To fall among the good is worthy praise: 80
And if the beauteous star which guides these eyes
   Were not by distance taken from my view,
   Which hath my soul inflamed,
Light should I count the burden I endure:
   But so this inward fire
   Already hath consumed the bones and nerves,
That Death upon my breast hath placed the key.
   Hence though I may have erred,
Months have revolved long since I were forgiven,
   If error dies provided man repent.   90

My song, forbid that man should touch thy robes,
   To see what beauteous lady does conceal:
   Let what is shown suffice;
Refuse to all the sweet and envied fruit
   For which each hand is stretched;
And should it happen that thou ever find'st
A friend of virtue, and he thee entreat,
   Robe thee in colours new;
Then show thyself, and make all loving hearts
Desire the flower of outward form so fair.   100

Doglia mi reca ne lo core ardire

Grief brings a daring spirit to my heart,
    To aid the will, which is the friend of truth:
    If therefore in my verse
    Are words that seem to censure all mankind,
    Ladies, be not surprised,
    But learn to know your own perverse desire;
    For beauty, which is yours by Love's consent,
    By his desire of old,
    Was formed to wait on virtue, and none else
    'Gainst which decree you sin.   10
    To you, who are enamoured then, I say:
    If beauty hath to you,
    Virtue to us, been given,
    And power to Love to form of two but one,
    You rightly cannot love,
    But ought to hide all beauty you possess;
    For virtue was its aim, and is not yours.
    Alas! where tends my strain?
    I say, the scorn were just,
    Noble and rightly praised, in lady who   20
    Should cast away her beauty from her care.

Man from himself hath banished virtue far;
    Not man indeed, but beast resembling man:
    O God, how wonderful
    To wish to fall abased from lord to slave!
    Or worse, from life to death!
    Virtue is to her Maker still submiss,
    Obeys, and honour seeks to gain.
    O ladies, long as Love
    Enrols her of the glorious family   30
    Which grace his blissful court;
    Forth from the happy gates she goes with joy
    And to her lady hies;
    There sojourns joyfully;
    With joy her noble vassalage performs;
    In her short pilgrimage

Preserves, adorns, enriches what she finds;
And wars with Death till he excites no care.
O handmaid dear and pure,
In heaven thy mould was cast;   40
Thou only mak'st the noble, and this proves
That thou the treasure art which never fails.

Slave not of lord, but of a worthless slave,
The man becomes who from that lord withdraws.
Hear now, how dear he pays,
If you consider well the twofold loss,
Who strays from virtue's path:
So vile and wayward is this servile lord,
That the eyes which render light unto the mind,
Through him are firmly closed;   50
So that his slave behoves to follow one
Who seeks but foolishness.
And now, that you may profit by my song,
I will descend, and make
The structure and the parts
More simple, that the sense may be more clear;
For rarely, under veil,
Dark parables the understanding reach;
And hence with you my reasoning should be plain;
This for your good I do,   60
Surely not for my own;
That every slave of vice you may abhor:
For who delight us make us like themselves.

He who is slave of vice is like the man
Who follows swift his lord, and knows not where,
Along a rueful way:
So fares the miser in pursuit of wealth,
Which lords it over all:
The miser runs, but swifter flies his peace;
O blindness of the mind, which cannot see   70
The folly of thy will!
He strives incessantly to swell his hoard,
Doting on boundless wealth.
Behold it reached by Death, who levels all:

Now say, what is thy gain
Thou undone miser blind?
Reply, if thou art able: there is none.
A curse hath been thy couch,
Which oft deceived thee with such flattering dreams;
Accursed thy unprofitable store,   80
Less lost if given to dogs;
For late and early thou
Hast reaped, and fondly grasped with both thy hands,
That which so soon shall leave thee far away.

As wealth with thirst immoderate is heaped,
So with immoderate grasp it is retained:
This avarice compels
The many into bondage, and if one
Resist, 'tis with much pain.
Where art thou Death? Kind Fortune where art thou?   90
Why not let loose the miser's unspent heaps?
If done, – then who is heir?
I know not; for a sphere encircles us
Which writes our fate above.
The fault is Reason's which corrects him not.
Says he: I am not free?
Alas! what poor defence
Urged by a sovereign whom a slave commands!
The shame is doubled here;
If well you mark their ways at whom I point: 100
O beasts, false to yourselves, cruel to others,
Who see men wandering
Naked, o'er hills and fens,
Men from whose presence vice has fled afar;
And you your garments throw o'er dregs of earth.

Before the miser's face pure Virtue stands,
Who still invites her enemies to peace;
A polished lure she holds,
To entice him to her; but it little serves;
For still he shuns the bait;   110
Then after various turns, and many a call,
Such her concern for him, she throws the food;

But close he keeps his wings;
And if at length he comes, 'tis when she is gone,
So much he seems annoyed.
How gifts may be conferred, and yet not bring
Praise to the benefactor,
I wish that all should hear.
Some by delay, some by a vain parade,
Some by a sour brow, 120
Subvert the gift, by selling it so dear,
That he alone who buys can know the cost.
Ask you, if gifts can wound?
Ay, so that the receiver
Will after think refusal is less bitter:
Thus does the miser wound himself and others.

Ladies, to you I have unveiled one limb
Of a vile worthless race who court your love,
That they may meet your scorn;
But more deformed is that which is concealed, 130
Wherefore too foul to tell.
In every one is gathered every vice;
For concord is confounded in the world.
Love's verdant branches spring
From blissful root, and other bliss attract,
Like in degree of worth.
Hear now at what conclusion I arrive;
Never let her believe,
Who beauty deems a good,
That she is loved by persons such as these; 140
If beauty we account
Among our ills, believe it then she may,
When brutal appetite shall love be called.
Perish the lady who
Her beauty shall divorce
From natural goodness, and through such a cause,
And out of reason's garden trusts in Love.

My Song, not far from here a lady dwells,
A native of our land,
Fair, courteous, and discreet, 150

Invoked by all, and yet divulged to none:
When, giving her a name,
We call on Vanna, Bianca, or Cortese;
To her pursue thy way, modest and veiled;
First stay thy course with her,
To her first, undisguised,
Show what thou art and wherefore sent by me,
Then journey on wherever she commands.

Amor, da che convien pur ch' io mi doglia

Love, since my lamentions must have vent,
    That men may mark my words,
    And see how all my virtue is extinct,
    O give me wisdom with the will to weep;
      So that my unchained grief
      Be told in words as strong as what I feel.
    Thy will is that I die, to that I bend;
    But me who shall excuse, unless I tell
    All that thou mak'st me feel?
Who will believe the toils in which I am caught?   10
    But if thou giv'st me power of speech as great
    As is my torment, lord, then ere I die,
    Let not this cruel maid hear my complaint;
    For should she know what inwardly I feel,
    Pity would make her beauteous face less fair.

Fly from her where I will, 'tis vain; her form
    Imagination brings
    Swift to my mind as thought, which leads her there.
    The silly soul, ingenious to its harm,
      Paints her all loveliness
      And cruelty, inventing its own pain;   20
    Then gazes, and when filled with the desire,
    Which strongly by the eyes attracts to her,
    Is anger'd 'gainst itself,

For kindling fire, where it burns wretchedly.
What argument of reason can control
My thoughts, which as an inward tempest rage?
The anguish which the bosom cannot hold
Breathes from the lips, so that 'tis understood,
And even to the eyes gives their desert.   30

The pictured form, my enemy, remains
   Victorious and severe,
   And lords it o'er the freedom of the will;
She of herself enamoured, makes me seek
   The substance of this shade;
   As like to like is ever wont to flee.
I know that I am snow which seeks the sun:
But to resist is vain; like him I move
   Who, in another's power
Marches obediently where he is killed.   40
When I am near her, words I seem to hear
Which say: Haste, haste, this man thou shalt see die.
Then I look out on whom to call for aid;
And thus am led at pleasure of the eyes
Which most unjustly give me mortal wounds.

What I become when wounded thus, O Love,
   Thou canst relate, not I;
   Thou, the spectator of my lifeless state;
And though the soul return unto the heart,
   Knowledge and memory   50
From her were sever'd while she was divorced.
When I revive, and look upon the wound
By which I was undone when I was struck,
   No comfort can I find,
But every limb is shaken by my fear;
And the discoloured features testify
How great the lightning's force which fell on me;
For though by a sweet smile the shaft be thrown
Yet long the features darkened will remain,
Because the spirit cannot feel assured.   60

Thus hast thou used me, Love, amid the Alps,
   And in the river's vale,

Along whose shore thy strength I ever feel:
Living and dead thou treat'st me as thou wilt,
Thanks to the cruel light
Whose flashes are the harbingers of death.
Alas! no ladies here, no gentle minds
I see, in whom my sorrows cause regret.
If she be unconcerned,
Never from others can I hope for aid.   70
And this fair spirit banished from thy court,
O Love, regards no blow from shaft of thine:
Pride has a breast-plate given of such defence,
That every dart is blunted ere it pierce;
For heart so armed no weapon can offend.

My little mountain Song, thou goest thy way;
Haply, my city, Florence, thou wilt see,
Who 'gainst me bars her gates,
Stripped of all pity and devoid of love.
If thou within her walls shouldst enter, say: 80
My master can with you no more wage war;
There, whence I come, he by a chain is bound
So strong, that, should your cruelty relent,
Here to return he is no longer free.

From *The Divine Comedy*:

Paradise

CANTO 17

As came to Clymene, to be made certain
    Of that which he had heard against himself,
    He who makes fathers chary still to children,

Even such was I, and such was I perceived
    By Beatrice and by the holy light
    That first on my account had changed its place.

Therefore my Lady said to me: 'Send forth
    The flame of thy desire, so that it issue
    Imprinted well with the internal stamp;

Not that our knowledge may be greater made   10
    By speech of thine, but to accustom thee
    To tell thy thirst, that we may give thee drink.'

'O my beloved tree, (that so dost lift thee,
    That even as minds terrestrial perceive
    No triangle containeth two obtuse,

So thou beholdest the contingent things
    Ere in themselves they are, fixing thine eyes
    Upon the point in which all times are present,)

While I was with Virgilius conjoined
    Upon the mountain that the souls doth heal,   20
    And when descending into the dead world,

Were spoken to me of my future life
    Some grievous words; although I feel myself
    In sooth foursquare against the blows of chance.

On this account my wish would be content
    To hear what fortune is approaching me,
    Because foreseen an arrow comes more slowly.'

Thus did I say unto that selfsame light
    That unto me had spoken before; and even
    As Beatrice willed was my own will confessed   30

Not in vague phrase, in which the foolish folk
    Ensnared themselves of old, ere yet was slain
    The Lamb of God who taketh sins away.

But with clear words and unambiguous
    Language responded that paternal love,
    Hid and revealed by its own proper smile:

'Contingency, that outside of the volume
    Of your materiality extends not,
    Is all depicted in the eternal aspect.

Necessity however thence it takes not,   40
    Except as from the eye, in which 'tis mirrored;
    A ship that with the current down descends.

From thence, e'en as there cometh to the ear
    Sweet harmony from an organ, comes in sight
    To me the time that is preparing for thee.

As forth from Athens went Hippolytus,
    By reason of his step-dame false and cruel,
    So thou from Florence must perforce depart.

Already this is willed, and this is sought for;
    And soon it shall be done by him who thinks it,   50
    Where every day the Christ is bought and sold.

The blame shall follow the offended party
    In outcry as is usual; but the vengeance
    Shall witness to the truth that doth dispense it.

Thou shalt abandon everything beloved
    Most tenderly, and this the arrow is
    Which first the bow of banishment shoots forth.

Thou shalt have proof how savoureth of salt
    The bread of others, and how hard a road
    The going down and up another's stairs.   60

And that which most shall weigh upon thy shoulders
    Will be the bad and foolish company
    With which into this valley thou shalt fall;

For all ingrate, all mad and impious
    Will they become against thee; but soon after
    They, and not thou, shall have the forehead scarlet.

Of their bestiality their own proceedings
    Shall furnish proof; so 'twill be well for thee
    A party to have made thee by thyself.

Thine earliest refuge and thine earliest inn   70
    Shall be the mighty Lombard's courtesy,
    Who on the Ladder bears the holy bird,

Who such benign regard shall have for thee
    That 'twixt you twain, in doing and in asking,
    That shall be first which is with others last.

With him shalt thou see one who at his birth
    Has by this star of strength been so impressed,
    That notable shall his achievements be.

Not yet the people are aware of him
    Through his young age, since only nine years yet   80
    Around about him have these wheels revolved

But ere the Gascon cheat the noble Henry,
    Some sparkles of his virtue shall appear
    In caring not for silver nor for toil.

So recognised shall his magnificence
    Become hereafter, that his enemies
    Will not have power to keep mute tongues about it.

On him rely, and on his benefits;
    By him shall many people be transformed;
    Changing condition rich and mendicant;   90

And written in thy mind thou hence shalt bear
    Of him, but shalt not say it' – and things said he
    Incredible to those who shall be present.

Then added: 'Son, these are the commentaries
    On what was said to thee; behold the snares
    That are concealed behind few revolutions;

Yet would I not thy neighbours thou shouldst envy,
　　　Because thy life into the future reaches
　　　Beyond the punishment of their perfidies.'

When by its silence showed that sainted soul   100
　　　That it had finished putting in the woof
　　　Into that web which I had given it warped,

Began I, even as he who yearneth after,
　　　Being in doubt, some counsel from a person
　　　Who seeth, and uprightly wills, and loves:

'Well see I, father mine, how spurreth on
　　　The time towards me such a blow to deal me
　　　As heaviest is to him who most gives way.

Therefore with foresight it is well I arm me,
　　　That, if the dearest place be taken from me,   110
　　　I may not lose the others by my songs.

Down through the world of infinite bitterness,
　　　And o'er the mountain, from whose beauteous summit
　　　The eyes of my own Lady lifted me,

And afterward through heaven from light to light,
　　　I have learned that which, if I tell again,
　　　Will be a savour of strong herbs to many.

And if I am a timid friend to truth,
　　　I fear lest I may lose my life with those
　　　Who will hereafter call this time the olden.'   120

The light in which was smiling my own treasure
　　　Which there I had discovered, flashed at first
　　　As in the sunshine doth a golden mirror;

Then made reply: 'A conscience overcast
　　　Or with its own or with another's shame,
　　　Will taste forsooth the tartness of thy word,

But ne'ertheless, all falsehood laid aside,
    Make manifest thy vision utterly,
    And let them scratch wherever is the itch;

For if thine utterance shall offensive be   130
    At the first taste, a vital nutriment
    'Twill leave thereafter, when it is digested.

This cry of thine shall do as doth the wind,
    Which smiteth most the most exalted summits,
    And that is no slight argument of honour.

Therefore are shown to thee within these wheels,
    Upon the mount and in the dolorous valley,
    Only the souls that unto fame are known;

Because the spirit of the hearer rests not,
    Nor doth confirm its faith by an example   140
    Which has the root of it unknown and hidden,

Or other reason that is not apparent.'

CANTO 26

While I was doubting for my vision quenched,
    Out of the flame refulgent that had quenched it
    Issued a breathing, that attentive made me,

Saying: 'While thou recoverest the sense
    Of seeing which in me thou hast consumed,
    'Tis well that speaking thou shouldst compensate it.

Begin then, and declare to what thy soul
    Is aimed, and count it for a certainty,
    Sight is in thee bewildered and not dead;

Because the Lady, who through this divine   10
    Region conducteth thee, has in her look
    The power the hand of Ananias had.'

I said: 'As pleaseth her, or soon or late
    Let the cure come to eyes that portals were
    When she with fire I ever burn with entered.

The Good, that gives contentment to this Court,
    The Alpha and Omega is of all
    The writing that love reads me low or loud.'

The selfsame voice, that taken had from me
    The terror of the sudden dazzlement,   20
    To speak still farther put it in my thought;

And said: 'In verity with finer sieve
    Behoveth thee to sift; thee it behoveth
    To say who aimed thy bow at such a target.'

And I: 'By philosophic arguments,
    And by authority that hence descends,
    Such love must needs imprint itself in me;

For Good, so far as good, when comprehended
    Doth straight enkindle love, and so much greater
    As more of goodness in itself it holds;   30

Then to that Essence (whose is such advantage
    That every good which out of it is found
    Is nothing but a ray of its own light)

More than elsewhither must the mind be moved
    Of every one, in loving, who discerns
    The truth in which this evidence is founded.

Such truth he to my intellect reveals
    Who demonstrates to me the primal love
    Of all the sempiternal substances.

The voice reveals it of the truthful Author,   40
    Who says to Moses, speaking of Himself,
    "I will make all my goodness pass before thee."

Thou too revealest it to me, beginning
    The loud Evangel, that proclaims the secret
    Of heaven to earth above all other edict.'

And I heard say: 'By human intellect
    And by authority concordant with it,
    Of all thy loves reserve for God the highest.

But say again if other cords thou feelest,
    Draw thee towards Him, that thou mayst proclaim   50
    With how many teeth this love is biting thee.'

The holy purpose of the Eagle of Christ
    Not latent was, nay, rather I perceived
    Whither he fain would my profession lead.

Therefore I recommenced: 'All of those bites
    Which have the power to turn the heart to God
    Unto my charity have been concurrent.

The being of the world, and my own being,
    The death which He endured that I may live,
    And that which all the faithful hope, as I do,   60

With the forementioned vivid consciousness
    Have drawn me from the sea of love perverse,
    And of the right have placed me on the shore.

The leaves, wherewith embowered is all the garden
    Of the Eternal Gardener, do I love
    As much as he has granted them of good.'

As soon as I had ceased, a song most sweet
    Throughout the heaven resounded, and my Lady
    Said with the others, 'Holy, holy, holy!'

And as at some keen light one wakes from sleep   70
    By reason of the visual spirit that runs
    Unto the splendour passed from coat to coat,

And he who wakes abhorreth what he sees,
    So all unconscious is his sudden waking,
    Until the judgment cometh to his aid,

So from before mine eyes did Beatrice
    Chase every mote with radiance of her own,
    That cast its light a thousand miles and more.

Whence better after than before I saw,
    And in a kind of wonderment I asked   80
    About a fourth light that I saw with us.

And said my Lady: 'There within those rays
    Gazes upon its Maker the first soul
    That ever the first virtue did create.'

Even as the bough that downward bends its top
    At transit of the wind, and then is lifted
    By its own virtue, which inclines it upward,

Likewise did I, the while that she was speaking,
    Being amazed, and then I was made bold
    By a desire to speak wherewith I burned.   90

And I began: 'O apple, that mature
    Alone hast been produced, O ancient father,
    To whom each wife is daughter and daughter-in-law,

Devoutly as I can I supplicate thee
    That thou wouldst speak to me; thou seest my wish;
    And I, to hear thee quickly, speak it not.'

Sometimes an animal, when covered, struggles
    So that his impulse needs must be apparent,
    By reason of the wrappage following it;

And in like manner the primeval soul   100
    Made clear to me athwart its covering
    How jubilant it was to give me pleasure.

Then breathed: 'Without thy uttering it to me,
    Thine inclination better I discern
    Than thou whatever thing is surest to thee;

For I behold it in the truthful mirror,
    That of Himself all things parhelion makes,
    And none makes Him parhelion of itself.

Thou fain wouldst hear how long ago God placed me
    Within the lofty garden, where this Lady   110
    Unto so long a stairway thee disposed,

And how long to mine eyes it was a pleasure,
    And of the great disdain the proper cause,
    And the language that I used and that I made.

Now, son of mine, the tasting of the tree
    Not in itself was cause of so great exile,
    But solely the o'erstepping of the bounds.

There, whence thy Lady moved Virgilius,
    Four thousand and three hundred and two circuits
    Made by the sun, this Council I desired;   120

And him I saw return to all the lights
    Of his highway nine hundred times and thirty,
    Whilst I upon the earth was tarrying.

The language that I spake was quite extinct
    Before that in the work interminable
    The people under Nimrod were employed;

For nevermore result of reasoning
    (Because of human pleasure that doth change,
    Obedient to the heavens) was durable.

A natural action is it that man speaks;   130
    But whether thus or thus, doth nature leave
    To your own art, as seemeth best to you.

Ere I descended to the infernal anguish,
    El was on earth the name of the Chief Good,
    From whom comes all the joy that wraps me round;

Eli he then was called, and that is proper,
    Because the use of men is like a leaf
    On bough, which goeth and another cometh.

Upon the mount that highest o'er the wave
    Rises was I, in life or pure or sinful,   140
    From the first hour to that which is the second,

As the sun changes quadrant, to the sixth.'

CANTO 33

'Thou Virgin Mother, daughter of thy Son,
    Humble and high beyond all other creature,
    The limit fixed of the eternal counsel,

Thou art the one who such nobility
    To human nature gave, that its Creator
    Did not disdain to make himself its creature.

Within thy womb rekindled was the love,
    By heat of which in the eternal peace
    After such wise this flower has germinated.

Here unto us thou art a noonday torch   10
    Of charity, and below there among mortals
    Thou art the living fountain-head of hope.

Lady, thou art so great, and so prevailing,
    That he who wishes grace, nor runs to thee,
    His aspirations without wings would fly.

Not only thy benignity gives succour
    To him who asketh it, but oftentimes
    Forerunneth of its own accord the asking.

In thee compassion is, in thee is pity,
    In thee magnificence; in thee unites   20
    Whate'er of goodness is in any creature.

Now doth this man, who from the lowest depth
    Of the universe as far as here has seen
    One after one the spiritual lives, .

Supplicate thee through grace for so much power
    That with his eyes he may uplift himself
    Higher towards the uttermost salvation.

And I, who never burned for my own seeing
    More than I do for his, all of my prayers
    Proffer to thee, and pray they come not short,   30

That thou wouldst scatter from him every cloud
    Of his mortality so with thy prayers,
    That the Chief Pleasure be to him displayed.

Still farther do I pray thee, Queen, who canst
    Whate'er thou wilt, that sound thou mayst preserve
    After so great a vision his affections.

Let thy protection conquer human movements;
    See Beatrice and all the blessed ones
    My prayers to second clasp their hands to thee!'

The eyes beloved and revered of God,   40
  Fastened upon the speaker, showed to us
    How grateful unto her are prayers devout;

Then unto the Eternal Light they turned,
    On which it is not credible could be
    By any creature bent an eye so clear.

And I, who to the end of all desires
    Was now approaching, even as I ought,
    The ardour of desire within me ended.

Bernard was beckoning unto me, and smiling,
    That I should upward look; but I already   50
    Was of my own accord such as he wished;

Because my sight, becoming purified,
    Was entering more and more into the ray
    Of the High Light which of itself is true.

From that time forward what I saw was greater
    Than our discourse, that to such vision yields,
    And yields the memory unto such excess.

Even as he is who seeth in a dream,
    And after dreaming the imprinted passion
    Remains, and to his mind the rest returns not,   60

Even such am I, for almost utterly
    Ceases my vision, and distilleth yet
    Within my heart the sweetness born of it;

Even thus the snow is in the sun unsealed,
    Even thus upon the wind in the light leaves
    Were the soothsayings of the Sibyl lost.

O Light Supreme, that dost so far uplift thee
    From the conceits of mortals, to my mind
    Of what thou didst appear re-lend a little,

And make my tongue of so great puissance,   70
    That but a single sparkle of thy glory
    It may bequeath unto the future people;

For by returning to my memory somewhat,
    And by a little sounding in these verses,
    More of thy victory shall be conceived!

I think the keenness of the living ray
    Which I endured would have bewildered me,
    If but mine eyes had been averted from it;

And I remember that I was more bold
    On this account to bear, so that I joined   80
    My aspect with the Glory Infinite.

O grace abundant, by which I presumed
    To fix my sight upon the Light Eternal,
    So that the seeing I consumed therein!

I saw that in its depth far down is lying
    Bound up with love together in one volume,
    What through the universe in leaves is scattered

Substance, and accident, and their operations,
    All interfused together in such wise
    That what I speak of is one simple light.   90

The universal fashion of this knot
    Methinks I saw, since more abundantly
    In saying this I feel that I rejoice.

One moment is more lethargy to me,
    Than five and twenty centuries to the emprise
    That startled Neptune with the shade of Argo!

My mind in this wise wholly in suspense,
    Steadfast, immovable, attentive gazed,
    And evermore with gazing grew enkindled.

In presence of that light one such becomes,   100
    That to withdraw therefrom for other prospect
    It is impossible he e'er consent;

Because the good, which object is of will,
    Is gathered all in this, and out of it
    That is defective which is perfect there.

Shorter henceforward will my language fall
    Of what I yet remember, than an infant's
    Who still his tongue doth moisten at the breast.

Not because more than one unmingled semblance
    Was in the living light on which I looked,   110
    For it is always what it was before;

But through the sight, that fortified itself
    In me by looking, one appearance only
    To me was ever changing as I changed.

Within the deep and luminous subsistence
    Of the High Light appeared to me three circles,
    Of threefold colour and of one dimension,

And by the second seemed the first reflected
    As Iris is by Iris, and the third
    Seemed fire that equally from both is breathed.   120

O how all speech is feeble and falls short
    Of my conceit, and this to what I saw
    Is such, 'tis not enough to call it little!

O Light Eterne, sole in thyself that dwellest,
    Sole knowest thyself, and, known unto thyself
    And knowing, lovest and smilest on thyself!

That circulation, which being thus conceived
    Appeared in thee as a reflected light,
    When somewhat contemplated by mine eyes,

Within itself, of its own very colour   130
    Seemed to me painted with our effigy,
    Wherefore my sight was all absorbed therein.

As the geometrician, who endeavours
    To square the circle, and discovers not,
    By taking thought, the principle he wants,

Even such was I at that new apparition;
    I wished to see how the image to the circle
    Conformed itself, and how it there finds place;

But my own wings were not enough for this,
    Had it not been that then my mind there smote   140
    A flash of lightning, wherein came its wish.

Here vigour failed the lofty fantasy:
    But now was turning my desire and will,
    Even as a wheel that equally is moved,

The Love which moves the sun and the other stars.

Notes

To every heart The opening sonnet of Dante's youthful work, the *New Life* from which the first 10 poems are taken.

Song, 'tis my will A ballad. The first poem of the *New Life* definitely addressed to Beatrice.

Even as the others mock From chapter 14 of the *New Life*: Beatrice's greeting is withheld.

Ladies that have intelligence in love A canzone; it marks a turning point in the *New Life* and the inauguration of the praise style. The poem is used to identify Dante in *Purgatory* 24: 51.

Love and the gentle heart This sonnet follows the one above; it is a tribute to Guido Guinizelli who, in his canzone *Al cor gentil rempaira sempre amore*, links love to nobility of heart, not of lineage. Guinizelli's first four lines read: Love always returns straight to the gentle heart/ Like a bird in the wood flies to the greenery;/ Neither was love made before the gentle heart,/ Nor was the gentle heart before love by nature formed . . .

My lady carries love This sonnet follows the two above; it is typical of Dante's praise style.

A very pitiful lady From the *New Life* chapter 23, this canzone is a tormented premonition of Beatrice's death; it is cast as an apocalyptic vision with elements recalling the crucifixion.

My lady looks so gentle & **For certain he hath seen** This sonnet and its pair are from the *New Life* chapter 26; both are praise poems.

Beyond the sphere The last poem of the *New Life*; Beatrice is by now dead and grief recedes. **The sphere which spreads to widest space:** the last of the nine concentric spheres which make up the Dantean Universe. The eight heavens of the Moon, Mercury, Venus, the Sun, Mars, Jupiter, Saturn and the Fixed Stars are bounded by the last heaven, the Primum Mobile, whose revolutions move all the others. Beyond this is the Empyrean where God dwells, outside time and space.

Canto 3 The words that inaugurate canto 3 are carved into Hell gate through which Dante passes from the borderlands into Hell itself. Set in the year 1300, Dante's journey through the afterlife (Hell, Purgatory, Heaven) probably starts on the evening of Maundy Thursday – 7 April that year. Dante enters through the gate the following day, Good Friday; his journey through Hell coincides with the time that Christ was in the tomb, and lasts until the evening of Saturday 9th April. The Underworld is a conical hole caused by the fall of Lucifer; it is concealed under Jerusalem and its apex, where Satan is trapped, is the deepest point of a spherical globe. But the sinners here are not yet within Hell either, for they are on the far side of the river Acheron. Always uncommitted in life, neither Heaven nor Hell accept them and they are now condemned to follow a whirling banner. Stung on by wasps and insects, their tears and blood feed a sea of maggots – part of the perverted ecology of the infernal world.

v. 50: him who made . . . possibly Pope Celestine V who abdicated after five months. **v. 64: Acheron . . .** Dante places this river at the edge of the realm of the dead as it would have been in classical myth. **v. 77: Charon . . .** The mythological ferryman of souls whom Dante demonises in this account; compare Virgil, *Aeneid* VI 298–304.

Canto 15 It is now Saturday 9th April; Dante and Virgil have descended to the seventh level where the violent are punished. They find themselves on a plain of burning sand on to which fire falls *like snow in the mountains without a wind* (*Hell* 14: 30). Dante is protected by the steam that rises from another of Hell's rivers, the Phlegethon, by whose banks he walks. Here he meets his teacher, Brunetto Latini whose characterisation, condemnation of Florence and prophecy of Dante's exile (see *Paradise*, Canto 17), have made the canto famous. The 'prophecy' of exile is possible because of the back-dating of the poem to 1300.

v. 26: Are you here . . . Brunetto Latini, b. c. 1220, d. c. 1294; orator, poet and notary public. Brunetto was a Guelph and like Dante later on, was also exiled. During this period, in France, he wrote an encylopaedic work, the *Tresor*. He lectured in rhetoric and wrote a collection of poems (the *Tesoretto*) in the vernacular: Dante counted him one of the *viri famosi*, as formative of the Italian language as poets like Guittone and Bonagiunta.

v. 86: another text as well . . . Dante may be referring to either of two prophecies delivered to him by sinners he has met previously: *Hell* 6: 64ff and 10: 79. **v.105: this one crime . . .** These sinners, described elsewhere as the violent against God (*Hell* 12: 46), are, by a tradition arising from 12: 51, known as sodomites. There is little evidence for this however among the characters that people this canto. **v. 106: Priscian . . .** probably the great grammatician of the sixth century. **v. 107: Francesco d'Accorso . . .** 1225–1294 an academic: lectured at the law school in Bologna and held the Chair at Oxford. **v. 109: One whom . . .** Probably Andrea de' Mozzi, Bishop of Florence until 1295 when the Pope ('the Servant of Servants'), Boniface VIII, moved him to Vicenza where he died the following year.

Canto 33 This is the penultimate canto of *Hell*. Dante and Virgil have descended to the ninth and lowest circle where the traitors are punished, encased, to varying degrees, in the frozen lake formed by the river Cocytus. Count Ugolino gnaws the back of Ruggieri's head taking eternal revenge on the Archbishop who had him, two sons and two grandsons starved to death in a tower in Pisa.
vv. 86–87: Uguccione, Brigata . . . respectively son and grandson of Ugolino; the other two are Gaddo (v. 63) and Anselmo (v. 48). **v. 113: Fra Alberigo . . .** murdered members of his own family at a feast to which he invited them (2 May 1285). He is therefore confined to the region of the ninth circle reserved for those who betray their guests, Ptolomea (v. 119). Still alive in the Spring of 1300, his horrendous crime ensures he joins the ranks of the undead (vv. 124–127). **v. 132: Branca d'Oria . . .** A Genoese nobleman and son-in-law to Michael Zanche (v. 140) whom he treacherously invites to a banquet and murders – with the help of another relation. Fra Alberigo suggests both are undead.

Wisdom and courtesy The last in a series of epistolary poems between Dante da Maiano and Dante. Love encourages in the lover virtues of moral, aesthetic and social benefit.

Remembrance Canzone; **v. 19:** the Italian reads, *ché non pur lui, ma suo onor difende*. The English might be better rendered, *For his own honour he defends, not only him* (i.e. the servant, v. 18).

Guido Written in the style of a Provençal pleasure poem (*plazer*), the sonnet conjures a feel-good fantasy, the poets of the new style gathered on a mystic, chivalric quest. Guido Cavalcanti and Lapo Gianni are poets.

By reason of a garland fair In the style of a Sicilian ballad; displays the other side of Cavalcanti's influence on Dante.

He whom you carry This is also one of the early *rime* from which the poems of the *New Life* were subsequently selected.

Forth from my lady's eyes & **Into thy hands** Two sonnets, Cavalcantian in style. For *Into thy hands* vv. **1 and 7–8**, see Luke 23: 46 and 1: 38.

A gentle train of ladies & **Upon a day** Both poems of the early *rime*. These two sonnets mark opposite extremes of experience and attitude. The first is a praise poem; *Upon a day* however, might well have found a place in the *New Life* to mark Beatrice's death. **v. 6: like a Greek** . . . traditionally an arrogant people.

The Banquet The first canzone of Dante's encyclopaedic work *The Banquet*. The **third heaven** is the heaven of Venus; those who move it are the heavenly Intelligences who, able to contemplate God directly, make manifest, or materially realise, his Idea – in this case the forces, emotional and otherwise, associated with Venus. Originally written in 1293; the canzone is also quoted by Charles Martel in the heaven of Venus (*Par* 8: 37).

Love This canzone opens the third treatise of *The Banquet*. As in the poem that precedes it, the central female figure is allegorical, but the poet nevertheless evokes elements essential to the praise style of his earlier poetry: the impossibility of properly describing the lady, her almost supernatural greatness, her capacity to morally and spiritually re-make her admirers. The poem is sung by Casella in *Purgatory* 2: 112.

The pleasant rhymes of Love The canzone inaugurates the fourth book of the unfinished *Banquet*. The poem applies courtly values to questions of nobility, of civic practicalities, of communal living – all issues with which the prose commentary is concerned. Guinizelli's poem (see note to *Love and the gentle heart*) and another by Guittone (*Non ver lingaggio fa sangue, ma core*) are almost certainly behind this doctrinal text.

Canto 5 & **Canto 6** It is now Easter day and Dante and Virgil have arrived on the lower slopes of Purgatory, an island-mountain in the middle of the southern seas. It is formed from the earth displaced by the fall of Lucifer, and like Hell, is divided into three main regions. This is Antepurgatory where the souls of the late penitents must wait before beginning their purgation. **v. 3: Pointing the finger** ... In the sun, Dante casts a shadow clearly advertising his corporeal state. **v. 63: he began** ... The soul who speaks here is Iacopo del Cassero assassinated in 1298 by hitmen hired by the Marquis of Ferrara, Azzo VIII. He is buried in Fano. **v. 88 Giovanna** ... Buonconte's widow whose prayers might have shortened his time in Antepurgatory. **v. 106: But of the other, other rule I make** ... Buonconte (a Ghibelline captain who died in the battle of Campaldino 11 June 1289 – v. 87) has repented at the last moment (vv. 97–98); the devil is left only his body ('the other') and tumbles it away in a storm so it may never have proper burial (v. 91). **v. 131: Pia** ... Was probably murdered by her husband, Nello d'Inghiramo dei Pannocchieschi, Lord of the Castello di Pietra in the Maremma (v. 132), so that he could marry another woman, Margherita Aldobrandeschi. Nello was still living in 1322.

Canto 6 finds Dante still among the same souls now crowding round him, begging him to take news back so that prayers the living pray will hasten them to their purgation. **vv. 14–24: Arezzo ... Brabant** ... 'Arezzo': a thirteenth-century judge who condemned to death a brother and uncle of Ghino di Tacco (v. 15) for violence and highway robbery. The latter had him killed in revenge – by decapitation in his own court-room at Rome. 'Him beside', Guccio dei Tarlati, a Ghibelline drowned in the Arno while fighting the Guelphs. 'Frederick Novello', killed in 1289 (or 1291), stretches out his hands to command Dante's attention. 'Of Pisa he' probably Gano, son of 'good Marzuco' (v. 19), assassinated by Ugolino (see *Hell* 33). Marzuco, by this time a Franciscan, resisted every impulse to vengeance. 'Count Orso' murdered by members of his family in 1286 (see also *Hell* 32: 55–60). 'Peter de la Brosse' chamberlain to Philip the Bold accused Mary of Brabant, the King's second wife, of murdering Louis, the King's eldest son by a first marriage. The Lady of Brabant got her revenge in 1278 when Peter was condemned to death for treachery. **v. 29: O thou, my luminary** ... Virgil; Dante's guide explains to him that prayers and indulgences do not contradict or change divine judgment. **v. 57: Him back returning** ... The sun – though now behind the hill so that Dante no longer casts a shadow. **v. 62: O thou Lombard spirit!** ... Sordello (b. c. 1200, d. c. 1273), a poet, like Virgil, and born like him, near Mantua. **vv. 107–108: the Capulets and** ... More political factions than families as in Shakespeare. Dante imagines himself a guide to the Holy Roman Emperor ('German Albert', of Hapsburg (v. 98), reigned 1298–1308) and uses the names to paint a picture of the divisions between imperialist and anti-imperialist factions respectively, which in the absence of positive leadership, had riven the whole of Lombardy. The Monaldi and the Philippeschi symbolise the same internecine and self-serving struggle between Guelph and Ghibelline in Orvieto: cities in Italy are all 'o'er-thronged/ With tyrants' (vv. 126–127).

Canto 26 It is now the Tuesday of Easter Week. Dante and Virgil have reached the seventh and final level of Purgatory where the lustful are punished in 'refining flame'. The sinners are divided into two groups (like ants or 'emmets'). The second group, guilty of unnatural lusts, travels from right to left; in Purgatory, everyone else moves from left to right. The protagonists in this canto are love poets. **v. 13: O thou who follow-est ...** The speaker is Guido Guinizelli (c. 1235–1276), celebrated by Dante in the sonnet from the *New Life*, 'Love and the gentle heart ...' **v. 109: there is one whose mother speech ...** The mother tongue, or vernacular as opposed to Latin – of another poet, Arnaut Daniel (Arnault) a Provençal troubadour; active second half of the twelfth century. **v. 113: the songster of Limoges ...** Giraut de Bornelh, troubadour, flourished c. 1220. **v. 118: Guittone ...** d'Arezzo, poet, b. c. 1230, d. c. 1294. **v. 123 far as needs ...** The Our Father up to but not including 'Lead us not into temptation ...'. **v. 132: Thy courtesy ...** Arnaut speaks in his native Provençal which is here translated.

Ye who are able A ballad. **v. 15: that gentle Lord ...** Love.

Ye words of mine & **Sweet rhymes** The poet complains of the unresponsiveness of his beloved; *Sweet rhymes* works as palinode to *Ye words*.

Two ladies Celebrating both beauty and virtue, the sensual and the moral, the sonnet is part of Dante's phase as moral poet.

Ladies, behold One of what are known as the *pargoletta* poems after the 'maiden fair and young' who may herself be an allegorical invention; (see next poem).

I feel the mighty power Restates courtly and stilnovist themes; probably an allegorical canzone, perhaps for the *pargoletta* (see above).

The circling year's First of the *rime petrose* (the stony rhymes), written in a harsh style and also known as the *rime per la donna pietra* (poems for the

Lady of stone). The *rime petrose* succeed the sweet new style and can be seen as the predecessors of the harsh language of *Hell*.

To the dim light Like the other *petrose*, this poem was probably composed between 1296–1298. It is a sestina, written in imitation of Arnaut Daniel's compositions (see *Purgatory*, Canto 26).

Severe shall be my speech Sweetness of style, sound and image are replaced by a *stile aspro* (a bitter or harsh style).

Three ladies & **Grief brings a daring spirit** Both these canzoni were written in exile, perhaps around 1302–1304. The three ladies and Dante all suffer banishment; a parallel is drawn between the private and the public situations. **vv. 16–18:** the 'friend' is Dante, the 'mansion' is his heart. **vv. 34–36:** Love's mother is Venus; Venus' sister, the speaker here, is Rectitude or Universal Justice. **vv. 50–54: 'I brought forth her . . . this other'** *ius gentium* and *lex humana*, the law of nations and positive law. **v. 59: a dart of either kind . . .** the golden arrow of Good and the leaden arrow of Evil. **vv. 81–82:** Dante refers here to his exile from Florence.

Love, since my lamentations Also known as the *montanina* (mountain song) because of its coda or *congedo*. Composed c. 1307 and sent with an accompanying commentary-letter to Count Moroello Malaspina (*Epistle* IV). The poem may relate a sudden passion Dante conceived for a woman in the Casentino.

Canto 17 Dante is now in Paradise, guided by his life's love, Beatrice. The fifth heaven (Mars) in which *Paradiso* 17 is set, is filled with souls who fought to the death for their fate. It is here that Dante meets his great-great-grandfather Cacciaguida (b. c. 1090, d. c. 1147), who delivers, at this midway point of the last canticle of the *Comedy*, the most detailed prophecy of Dante's coming exile. **v. 1: As came to Clymene . . .** Phaethon has been told that Apollo is not his father and approaches his mother about the matter. To convince him of his paternity, Apollo lets Phaethon drive the chariot of the Sun in which Phaethon crashes to his death. **vv. 46–47: As forth from Athens . . .** Hippolytus is exiled under false charges of fraud brought by his step-mother, Phaedra. Dante is drawing attention to the parallel with his own exile brought about by false accusation. **v. 71: the mighty Lombard's courtesy . . .** Bartolomeo della Scala (d. 7 March 1304) to whose court in Verona Dante first repaired in 1303. His younger brother Cangrande (born in 1291 and therefore nine years old in 1300 – v. 80) became Lord of Verona in 1312 and Dante stayed with him until 1318. **v. 82: ere the Gascon** ... Pope Clement V who first supported, then abandoned Henry VII in his Italian campaign. **v. 110: the dearest place** ... Florence.

Canto 26 In the eighth heaven, of the fixed stars, Dante is examined on the three theological virtues, Faith, Hope, Love, by Peter, James and John respectively. Canto 26 contains the examination on Love and the meeting with the first human, Adam, whom Dante sees when Beatrice restores the sight he lost by gazing too intently at St John's brightly shining soul (canto 25). **vv. 41–42: Who says to Moses** ... See Exodus 33: 18–23. **v. 44: The loud Evangel** ... John's Gospel, chapter 1 or the book of Revelation, traditionally attributed to him. **vv. 118–123:** Adam says he spent 4,302 years in Limbo before Christ liberated him in the Harrowing of Hell (v. 119); he lived for 930 years (vv. 122–123). **v. 125: the work interminable** ... is the construction of the Tower of Babel (Genesis 11: 1–9). **vv. 139–142: Upon the mount** ... Mount Purgatory, whose topmost level is the Earthly Paradise which Dante identifies with Eden. Adam says he spent six hours there, the time taken for the sun to move through one 'quadrant' or 90°.

Canto 33 In canto 33 the culmination of the poem and of the journey coincide. Here, finally, Dante meets God face to face. He is guided now by St Bernard who has replaced Beatrice (*Paradise* 31: 58ff). Bernard intercedes for Dante with the Virgin; only then (v. 55ff) is Dante granted direct vision of the Godhead.
v. 9: this flower ... the population of Heaven figure themselves and their hierarchy as a white rose (*Par* 30–32) whose arrays of different petals represent different kinds of people, born at different times – before, or after, Christ. **v. 96: That startled Neptune** ... The sea-god looks up to see the shadow of the Argo pass above him as the Argonauts sail to Colchis to steal the Golden Fleece. Dante took this event to have occurred 25 centuries previously; his own oneiric experience is, he implies, as difficult to hold in memory as it is to conserve a history 2,500 years old. **v. 119: As Iris is by Iris** ... the rainbow. Double rainbows, in which the second is formed by refraction and partial reflection, invert the order of the spectrum in the second arc.

Everyman's Poetry

Titles available in this series

William Blake
ed. Peter Butter
0 460 87800 X

The Brontës
ed. Pamela Norris
0 460 87864 6

**Rupert Brooke &
Wilfred Owen**
ed. George Walter
0 460 87801 8

**Elizabeth Barrett
Browning**
ed. Colin Graham
0 460 87894 8

Robert Browning
ed. Colin Graham
0 460 87893 X

Robert Burns
ed. Donald Low
0 460 87814 X

Lord Byron
ed. Jane Stabler
0 460 87810 7

Geoffrey Chaucer:
Comic and Bawdy Tales
ed. Malcolm Andrew
0 460 87869 7

John Clare
ed. R. K. R. Thornton
0 460 87823 9

Arthur Hugh Clough
ed. John Beer
0 460 87939 1

Samuel Taylor Coleridge
ed. John Beer
0 460 87826 3

Dante
ed. Anna Lawrence
0 460 87955 3

Emily Dickinson
ed. Helen McNeil
0 460 87895 6

John Donne
ed. D. J. Enright
0 460 87901 4

John Dryden
ed. David Hopkins
0 460 87940 5

Four Metaphysical Poets
ed. Douglas Brooks-Davies
0 460 87857 3

Oliver Goldsmith
ed Robert L. Mack
0 460 87827 1

Thomas Gray
ed. Robert L. Mack
0 460 87805 0

Ivor Gurney
ed. George Walter
0 460 87797 6

Thomas Hardy
ed. Norman Page
0 460 87956 1

Heinrich Heine
ed. T. J. Reed
& David Cram
0 460 87865 4

George Herbert
ed. D. J. Enright
0 460 87795 X

Robert Herrick
ed. Douglas Brooks-Davies
0 460 87799 2

John Keats
ed. Nicholas Roe
0 460 87808 5

Omar Khayyám
ed. Tony Briggs
0 460 87954 5

Rudyard Kipling
ed. Jan Hewitt
0 460 87941 3

**Henry Wadsworth
Longfellow**
ed. Anthony Thwaite
0 460 87821 2

Andrew Marvell
ed. Gordon Campbell
0 460 87812 3

John Milton
ed. Gordon Campbell
0 460 87813 1

More Poetry Please!
Foreword by P. J.
Kavanagh
0 460 87899 9

Edgar Allan Poe
ed. Richard Gray
0 460 87804 2

Poetry Please!
Foreword by
Charles Causley
0 460 87824 7

Alexander Pope
ed. Douglas Brooks-
Davies
0 460 87798 4

Alexander Pushkin
ed. A. D. P. Briggs
0 460 87862 X

Lord Rochester
ed. Paddy Lyons
0 460 87819 0

Christina Rossetti
ed. Jan Marsh
0 460 87820 4

William Shakespeare
ed. Martin Dodsworth
0 460 87815 8

Percy Bysshe Shelley
ed. Timothy Webb
0 460 87944 8

John Skelton
ed. Greg Walker
0 460 87796 8

R. L. Stevenson
ed. Jenni Calder
0 460 87809 3

Jonathan Swift
ed. Michael Bruce
0 460 87945 6

**Algernon Charles
Swinburne**
ed. Catherine Maxwell
0 460 87871 9

Alfred, Lord Tennyson
ed. Michael Baron
0 460 87802 6

Dylan Thomas
ed. Walford Davies
0 460 87831 X

Edward Thomas
ed. William Cooke
0 460 87877 8

R. S. Thomas
ed. Anthony Thwaite
0 460 87811 5

Walt Whitman
ed. Ellman Crasnow
0 460 87825 5

Oscar Wilde
ed. Robert Mighall
0 460 87803 4

William Wordsworth
ed. Stephen Logan
0 460 87946 4

W. B. Yeats
ed. John Kelly
0 460 87902 2

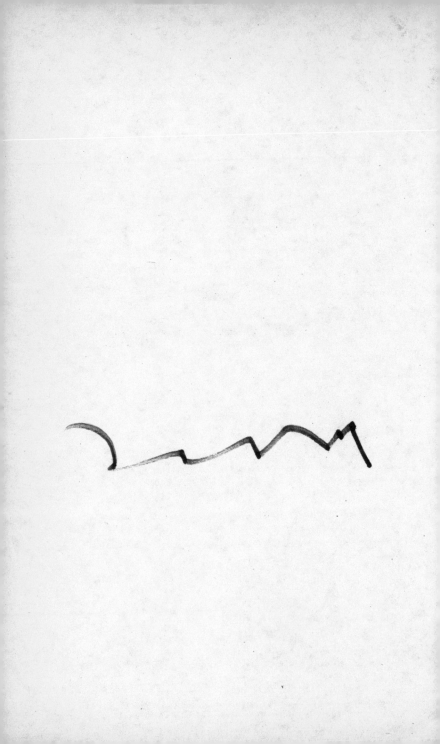